Contents

5 The Troubled Colossus
11 Building a Nation
31 The Cost of Expansion
47 Politicians and Reformers
63 Theodore Roosevelt and the Progressive Movement
79 The Positive President
93 America and the World
109 The Decline of Progressivism
119 The Legacy

Cover: Theodore Roosevelt playing all the roles—a caricature of the famous painting, 'The Spirit of '76'
Front endpaper: Contemporary French cartoon contrasts the rising sun of Theodore Roosevelt's America with the withered grandeur of the Old World
Rear endpaper: Monument raised in Washington Square, New York to celebrate the valour of the US Navy in the Spanish-American War of 1898

Copyright © 1971: A E Campbell
First published 1971 by BPC Unit 75
St Giles House 49 Poland St London W1
in the British Commonwealth and
American Heritage Press
551 Fifth Avenue New York NY 10017
in the United States of America
Library of Congress Catalogue Card
Number: 78-136174
Made and printed in Great Britain by
Purnell & Sons Ltd Paulton Somerset

AMERICA COMES OF AGE
The Era of Theodore Roosevelt

A E Campbell

St. Mary Regional High School
Library
310 Augusta Street
South Amboy, New Jersey 08879

St. Mary High School Library

9321

American Heritage Press
General Editor: John Roberts

Prologue
The Troubled Colossus

At the beginning of the 20th century the United States was, as today, deeply divided, and divided along several lines of cleavage. For some the future of the country seemed as promising as ever, the past mere prologue to glories yet to come. By every economic standard expansion continued. Already the United States was the world's leading industrial power, ahead of Germany and Britain and bound, it seemed, to move ahead still further. Her population continued to grow, stimulated by the immigrants who poured in from Europe as well as by natural growth, and with her population grew her wealth. It could only be a matter of time before she overhauled Britain in such areas as finance and international trade where Britain's early start still enabled her to hold a lead. Moreover, though part of America's success had to be set down to great natural resources, part also was the result of natural ingenuity. The Chicago Exposition of 1893, symbolically held in the nation's great central city, and that at Buffalo in 1900, had something of the effect of the Great Exhibition of 1851 in Britain on those who visited it. The technical marvels displayed were dazzling, but they held out the promise of more and more to come, in a progress to which there could be no end. The age of science fiction had begun, and then as now the men of fiction spoke less than the truth.

Optimists could find even more grounds for their optimism. The United States had just fought and easily won the Spanish-American War, depriving Spain of most of her remaining shreds of empire. It had been, as John Hay, Secretary of State, put it, 'a splendid little war'. To win it against a country so relatively small and backward as Spain had certainly been no great feat, and the defects of the American army had been revealed in the contest much as those of the British army were shown up by the Boers. But after all the United States had always lacked a military tradition and prided herself on lacking one. There had been little preparation for war — by Euro-

Left: 1865 — for the Northern states, victory: Union troops at Appomattox, Virginia, scene of the Confederate surrender

5

pean standards the whole affair had been improvised. When adequate allowance was made for this factor — and one could make as much or as little as one liked — America's victory showed what could be expected if the United States ever got down to fighting. At least Americans jealous for their country's standing in the world found plenty of support for their national pride from Europe. The powers there conducted their affairs without much reference to the United States, for the tradition of isolation was recognised and respected; but they were very careful not to offend the new colossus. An amiable giant enough, and not well armed; but not to be trifled with. That was the United States.

The growth of discontent
But not all Americans could be so cheerfully optimistic. Already it was becoming clear that the wealth of the country was very unevenly divided and, a subtler point, that the realisation of this imbalance was causing resentment. In some societies at some times, the poor have taken pride in the luxury, the glory, the ostentation of their rulers, even while they lived in poverty that their masters might live in wealth. But not in the late 19th-century United States. The problem of rich against poor was complicated by regional divisions. In 1896, the men of the West had dominated the Democratic Party, had put forward a Western spokesman, William Jennings Bryan, as candidate for President, and had voiced the grievances of Western farmers against the big city businessmen who had, they felt, the country in their grip. Although Bryan had been defeated, the struggle had been too close for comfort and had left bitterness behind.

Farmers were not the only discontented Americans. They had failed to find enough allies to win the election, but they had known where to look. Workers also were showing signs of discontent. The trade union movement was growing, and becoming more vigorous in its tactics and more intransigent in its demands. In the view of most modern historians, the unions behaved with great moderation and sobriety, and indeed, to all but the most die-hard, they were not very frightening even at the time. It was the implication of the movement rather than its immediate threat which caused concern, and which, to thoughtful men, linked unionised labour with farm discontent as a sinister portent. For, as John Mitchell, one of the miners' leaders, put it: 'The average wage-earner has made up his mind that he must remain a wage-earner. He has given up the hope of a kingdom to come, where he will be a capitalist, and he asks that the reward for his work be given to him as a working man.' Behind that comment could be seen not merely an attack

on wealth, but a challenge to the basic American ethos of self-improvement through individual effort, with financial independence as the proper goal.

Americans were not disposed to accept their discontents meekly. Theirs was a country in which anything that was wrong could be put right, in which energetic action was the answer to any problem. The energy, latent but apparent and apparently dangerous, of the deprived and underprivileged was indeed part of the problem. It called forth a corresponding energy on the part of reformers. The most characteristic of these were men who sympathised with many of the grievances they heard and saw—how else could they have been reformers?—but not with the most violent and radical remedies that were proposed. They believed that reform within the American tradition was possible and would be adequate. These were the men who came together to form what is called the Progressive movement, which gave its temper to the whole period with which this book is concerned. The Progressive movement became a political party only late in its history, and as a political party it was never successful. During its best and most successful years it was a movement in a much looser sense, so loose indeed that historians have differed strongly in their interpretations of its essential nature. It is not easy to say more than that a man was a Progressive if other Progressives agreed that he was one. Different Progressives concentrated on different evils. What seemed important to some seemed secondary to others. Some were far more radical than others; some were more optimistic than others. Yet it can be agreed that the Progressives were both reformers and conservatives. They wanted to reform in order to conserve. They did not regard American society as evil, least of all as worse than others. They supposed that when what was wrong had been put right, the result would be something recognisably American. Like any other group of reformers they have suffered from the passage of time. What they fought for now seems obvious; and what they overlooked or neglected seems obvious too, so that they now look more like conservatives than reformers. Yet reformers they were.

They had two main weapons. The first, obviously, was improved legislation, to close the loopholes which allowed certain evils to operate or to regulate areas in which regulation was needed. But it has often been true in America, as elsewhere, that evils are less the result of poor legislation than of the neglect of legislation by weak or corrupt officials. The second Progressive weapon was

Left: Northern victory ended slavery in the United States —Union soldiers stand guard outside a Virginia slave pen

7

improved public morality. More energy, courage, and public spirit on the part of good and intelligent men, the natural leaders of society, would deny power to the bad and corrupt, but plausible, cunning, and energetic men who would otherwise seize it. There was, clearly, a strong élitist stream in Progressive thinking, mingling with a strong democratic stream.

In the priority which they gave to legislation or leadership the Progressives differed, as they did about almost everything else. In few men was the tension between legislation and leadership so strong as in the key figure who has been chosen to give unity to this book. Theodore Roosevelt is not usually regarded by historians as one of the great Presidents. He is ranked rather with the best of those just less than great – below Washington, or Lincoln, or Franklin Roosevelt, or even his arch-rival, the man he hated, Woodrow Wilson. But great or not, in an extraordinary measure he had the capacity to sum up in his own person the feelings, the ideals, the ambitions, the hopes, and – sometimes – the fears of his countrymen. For historians he provides a superb test of the temper of his time. In many matters he failed, often because of his own failings. But he captured the heart of the American people as few have before or since. He was admired and he was loved. And he was laughed at, for there was always something slightly comic about Roosevelt. But the laughter was tolerant, affectionate laughter and not disrespectful, for 'TR' also had the qualities that Americans most admired. He was cocky, pugnacious, forthright, physically active, morally courageous – and not, perhaps, oversensitive. He was probably the last President to confess freely – and clearly truthfully – that he enjoyed his time in the White House. He had 'a bully time'. With such a man in charge, or even with such a man active in politics, there could not be much wrong. Something was always liable to happen, and it would probably be exciting. The personality of Roosevelt is one powerful reason why, for all its defects, many men could later look back to the period before the First World War as 'the good years'.

Right: *The white South was crushed: ruins of Columbia, South Carolina after the passage of Sherman's Union army* **(top).** *Both South and North suffered a further terrible blow at the end of the Civil War from the assassination of President Lincoln (contemporary magazine illustration of the martyred President's funeral procession* **(bottom)***). Before his death Lincoln had promised to work for the restoration of the nation 'with malice toward none; with charity for all'. But his successor, Andrew Johnson, was unable to resist demands that the South be punished for her secession by military occupation and the disenfranchisement of the leaders of the defeated Confederacy*

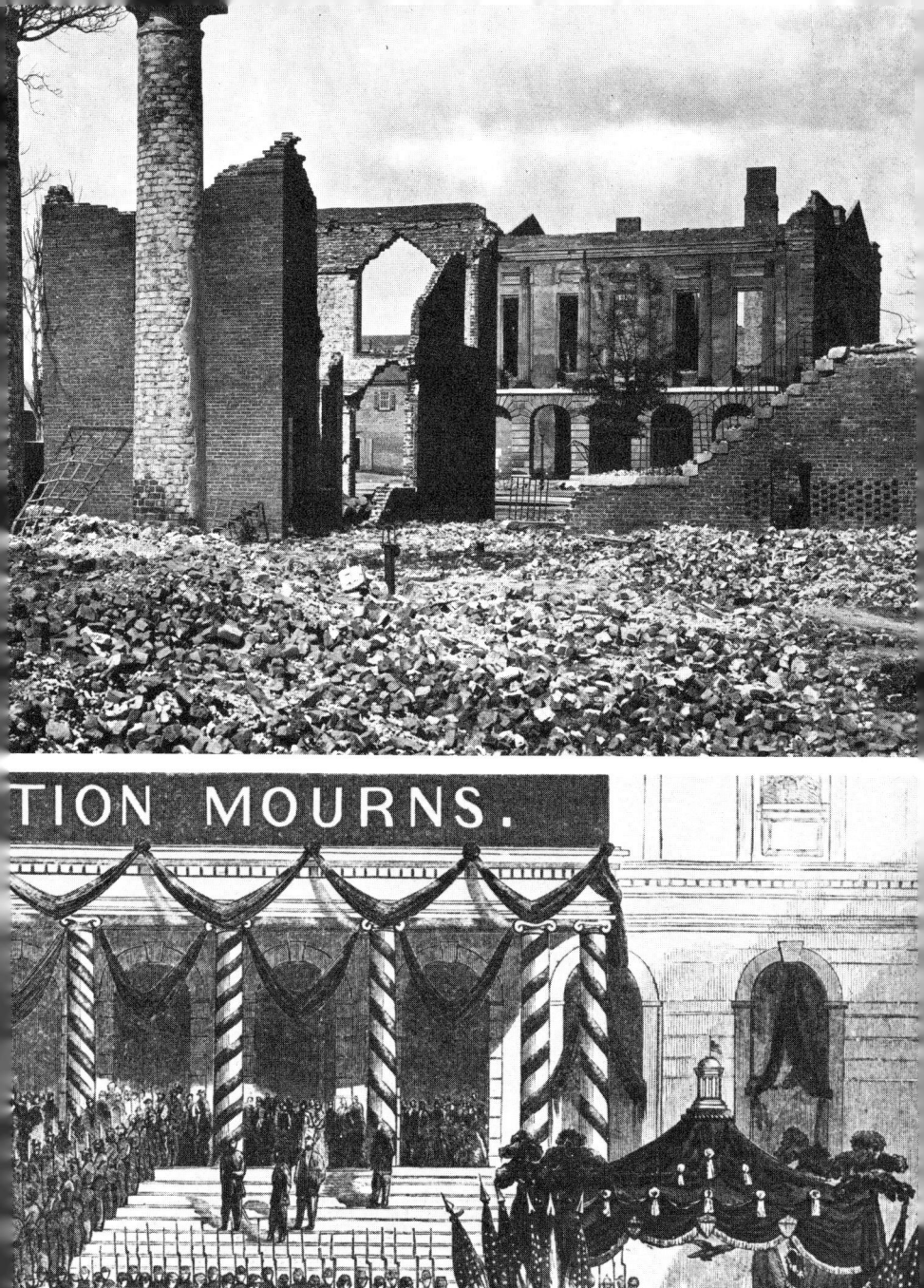

Chapter 1
Building a Nation

From the beginning of its history, the United States grew at an extraordinary speed; and from the start, the American people expected rapid growth and looked forward to it as something natural, inevitable, preordained. As their expectations were realized, so they were confirmed. Growth inevitably brought strains, but any account of American history must set growth, and the expectation of growth, in first place.

Two circumstances made the growth of America, at a pace beyond that of European states, possible and inevitable. The first was possession of a continent, almost empty, waiting to be developed and exploited, and defended by only a scattering of Indians, whose rights could be neglected or overborne. The other was a flow of immigrants from Europe, eager to develop and exploit this rich new land.

The main thrust of American expansion was always westwards. Even while Britain was still contending for control of North America with France and Spain, the thirteen British colonies, ranged down the eastern seaboard of the continent, grew far faster than their rivals. When those colonies won their independence in 1783, France had been defeated and Spain was in decline. From the outset the young United States was dominant in her continent. The first pioneers pushed up the eastern rivers, found passes through the mountains from which the rivers came, and spread into the regions beyond which drained into the Mississippi and the Great Lakes. Rather later, other settlers began to approach the country up the Mississippi itself and to move east and west from various points on the great river. The early settlers, chiefly of British descent, were joined about the middle of the 19th century by Irish, fleeing from the famine of the late 1840s, and by Germans, fleeing from the failure of their liberal revolution in 1848. And, of course, **14** ▷

Left: Late 19th-century allegory of the nation's westward progress. Now that the war was over, Americans were once again free to devote their full energies to the exploitation of their country. **Next page:** Railroads—engines of expansion

11

there were Negroes, who were legally transported as slaves over the dreadful 'middle passage' from West Africa until the trade was banned from the year 1808, and surreptitiously brought in even thereafter.

The settlement, the development, the expansion, were undertaken as private ventures. The share of government was confined to the very minimum of regulation and control. For this there were several reasons. First, the Americans had won their independence from a government which, so they had persuaded themselves, was despotic. It interfered to restrict their activities in ways which harmed and did not help them, and above all it taxed them for imperial purposes which they felt to be none of theirs. Suspicion of governmental tyranny was one of the legacies of the American Revolution. It is worth emphasising that the original American objection to British government was not that it was alien, but that it was despotic.

A quite different argument pointed to the same conclusion. Conservative Americans feared the power of the people almost as much as that of the King. They feared that the numerous poor, who had votes, would use them to plunder men of property. They feared that the poor, being also ignorant, would fall under the sway of demagogues who would flatter and bribe them. Despotism might be brought back by popular demand. Within the states, democracy could hardly be challenged. Conservatives hoped to check it by setting up a national government with some control over the states but with strictly limited powers of its own; a national government which was indirectly elected, and so partially sheltered from abrupt changes in the popular mood.

Such a government could only be created by agreement among the thirteen states, each of which had gained its own independence. Thus power passed to the federal government was, in a sense, power lost to the state governments. It received only those powers which the states chose to hand over. The delegates from the several states who gathered to draft a federal constitution accepted that there must be some restrictions on what the states could do. But even at that stage the states differed greatly in size and population, and their interests were divergent. The Constitution of the United States was the product of much compromise among men who were as anxious to protect the interests of existing states as they were to advance the interests of the new nation. A government established by such men was bound to be strictly limited.

Right: 'Go West, young man' urged the newspaperman Horace Greeley (1811-72) — millions, young and old, took his advice

The passing of the frontier

● Settled in 1870

● Settled 1870-1890

● Unsettled 1890 (under two people per square mile)

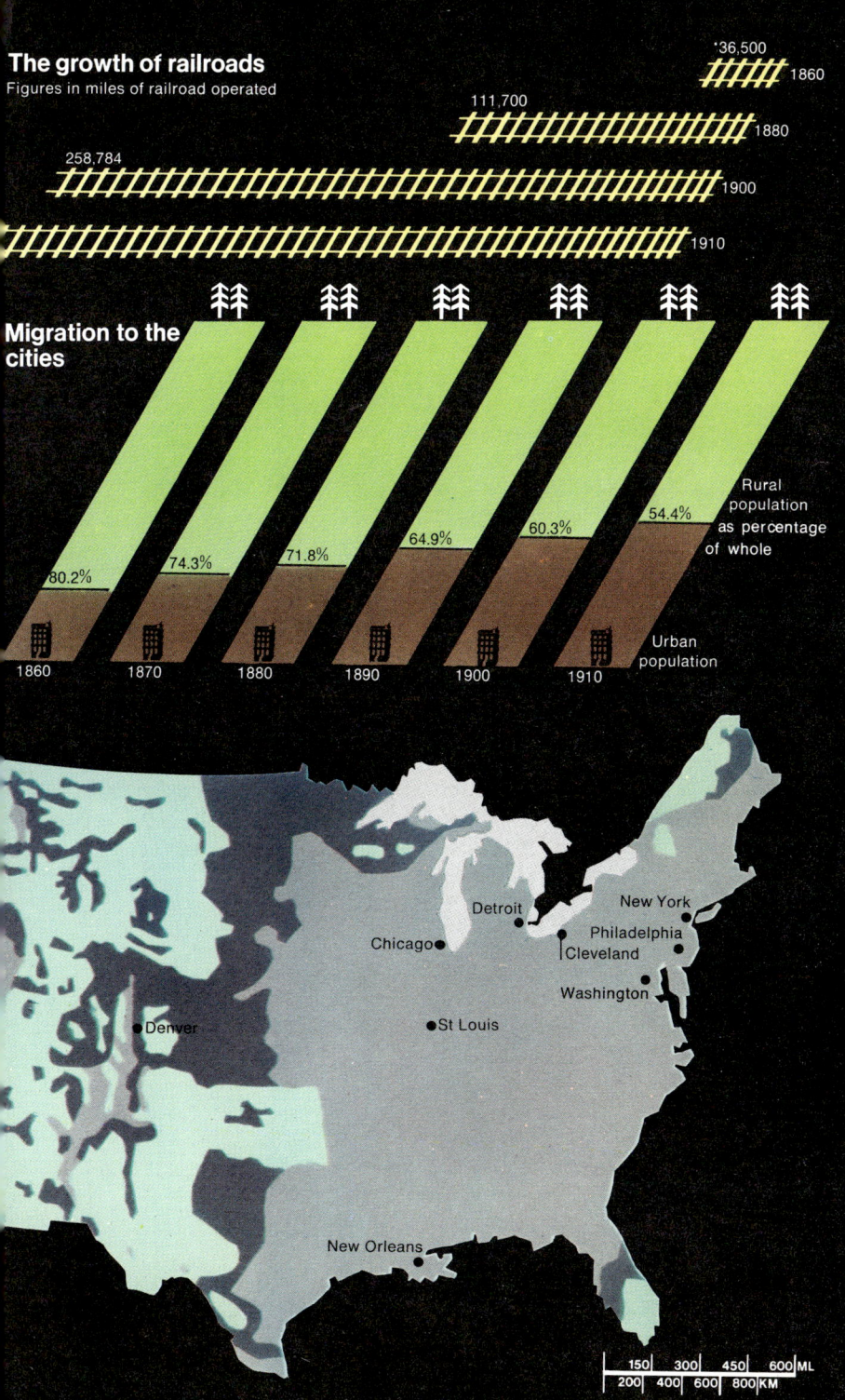

Though these reasons for limiting government seemed cogent, the passage of time did much to overcome them. As the country grew, so did American nationalism. As the 19th century advanced, tyranny seemed less likely and democracy less dangerous. Unhappily, however, Americans became increasingly divided by one problem which would brook no compromise—slavery. The Northern states, and the new states to the west, abandoned slavery; but it remained a flourishing institution in the South even after the importation of slaves had been made illegal. After 1800, cotton growing became more and more dominant in the economy of the South, and cotton was grown by slave labour on plantations, some very large, but most small. Southerners believed that their economy depended on slavery, but they clung to their institution also because they could see no way of co-existing with a large population of free Negroes. Northerners, whose states had few Negroes, were content to leave that problem to the South. They offered little constructive help in solving it.

Since each state had the power to establish its own domestic laws, there was no proper way in which anti-slavery men could use the national government to attack slavery in existing states, and they admitted as much. The abolitionists, who wanted to outlaw slavery at once, were never more than a small minority. But the country was expanding. As it did so, new states would be formed and given all the rights and powers of the older states. Once admitted as states, they could determine their own laws, and allow or ban slavery as they thought best. The admission of states, however, and the control of settlement in regions which were not yet states, were matters for the federal government. How should it act? In the end, the problem proved insoluble by any means short of civil war; but for some years it was kept under control by compromise and by inaction. The men who wanted the country free waited, in the well-founded belief that time was on their side. Slavery men, increasingly apprehensive, placed their hope in the strict limitation of federal power, and tried to establish the rule that slavery must not be attacked and must be allowed to expand.

So there were powerful reasons why men should distrust any increase in government. The sectional split over slavery was only the most obvious and most testing of several sectional divisions. When men could not agree on what the government should do, it was natural to agree that it should do almost nothing. Only one President in the early 19th century, John Quincy Adams,

Right: Men and machines conquered the West: harvesting on the great plains **(top)**; a party of travelling workers **(bottom)**

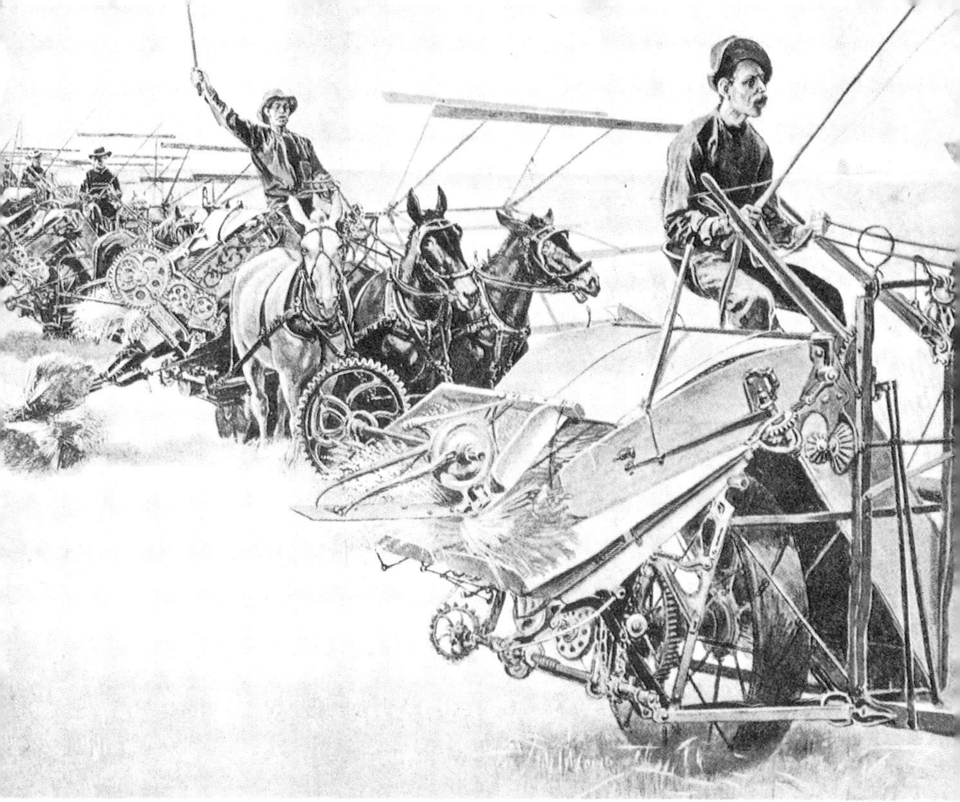

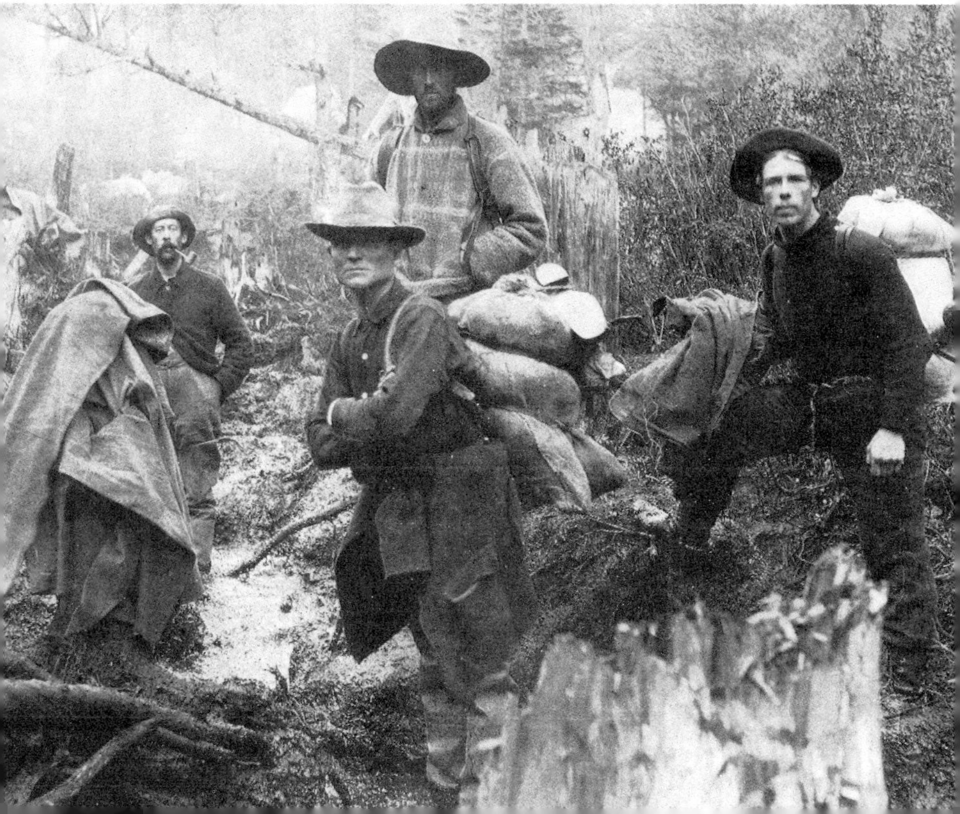

envisaged a programme of planned national expansion, and he had no success in persuading his countrymen to support such a programme. There were no compelling reasons for demanding an expansion of government power. Americans, having made their Constitution, did not find that they had made themselves a strait-jacket. If they had, they would have changed it, as they have done in more recent years, usually by reinterpretation rather than by formal modification. The attitudes which were written into the Constitution served them well, and so survived for many years. All the evidence suggested that the growth of the country would proceed by private enterprise. The settlers came as individuals, because they wanted to. They came because the opportunities for them were present in America. They needed nothing from the governments, whether federal or state, except permission to enter. In the first half of the 19th century, land which could profitably be worked by traditional European techniques, and by a farmer and his family, was waiting for the immigrant. In the absence of artificial restrictions, it was cheaply available.

The single most important positive need was for an adequate transport system. Here too the problem was on a scale which made solution easy. Roads and bridges could be built, later a canal system could be developed, and later still a railway network, through a system similar to that used in Britain, in which the role of government was essentially permissive. If private capital to finance a venture was forthcoming, that was taken as evidence of its social utility. Competition among the states for transport development and the prosperity which it brought was keen. State governments would grant the venture a charter and the right to acquire needed land. Sometimes they would themselves convey the land and add financial privileges of one sort or another. There has been no reluctance among Americans, then or at any other time, to make use of government; but what they wanted from governments was usually merely the right to act. The great era of canal building opened in 1825, when the Erie Canal linked the Great Lakes to New York. The canals were challenged by railways almost before they were built. The first railway company, the Baltimore and Ohio, was chartered in 1827, and by 1860 more than 30,000 miles of rail had been laid.

Even as this expansion continued, the political system began to break down. Though the Founding Fathers had deplored party politics, a national two-party structure had grown up during the early 19th century, the parties eventually taking the names Democratic and Whig. From about 1850 the Whig Party began to break up, essentially over the question of how to

Left: Mail order catalogue — the progressive farmer's friend

deal with the expansion of slavery into national territory which had not yet been formed into states. Sooner or later most of its Northern members moved over to the new Republican Party. The Democratic Party held together longer, but fell under Southern domination, as former Southern Whigs moved over to its ranks, while Northern Democrats drifted towards the Republicans. In 1860 Abraham Lincoln was elected President as the candidate of the Republican Party, whose chief object was to ensure that slavery should not expand into national territory. His election was strictly a sectional victory. The leaders of the Southern states rightly concluded that in the North hostility to slavery was permanent and growing; and, rightly or wrongly, decided that they must withdraw, while there was still time, from a Union in which they had no future. Eleven states seceded and formed a new union, the Confederacy. After a period of uneasy stalemate, fighting broke out in April 1861 when Confederate forces fired on Fort Sumter, a fort held by Union troops which commanded the harbour of Charleston, South Carolina's major port.

Effects of the war

Only two general points about the Civil War need be made here. Until late in the war Lincoln, as the spokesman for his section and his party, insisted that it was not a war to end slavery: it was a war only to compel rebels to return to their true allegiance. As the North ground its way to victory, it became increasingly clear that it would be intolerable for slavery to survive in a restored Union, and it was abolished almost without argument, ultimately by an amendment to the Constitution. Yet the whole course of the debate about slavery had isolated that single issue from others. The American Civil War was not, as civil wars commonly are, a contest between different views of what society should be. It was not even a struggle for power between rival social groups. When the Southern states seceded they were led by the men who had led them while they were in the Union. When they wrote a constitution for the nation they hoped to create, it followed in almost every respect the Constitution of the nation they had left. And when the Union was restored — under the old Constitution, with only the most limited changes — many of the same men were soon returned to place and power.

There was no intention, then, of changing or enlarging the functions of government. But, inevitably, during the course of the war, the power of the central government did increase. The Constitution makes the President,

19

among other things, the nation's Commander-in-Chief, and a shrewd politician, such as Lincoln undoubtedly was, can make effective use of that office in wartime. Yet, considering the length and savagery of the war, it is surprising how restricted the powers of government remained. Lincoln was perpetually under attack as a man bent on creating a despotism, though to the modern eye his powers look less than adequate. On the other side, the Confederate President, Jefferson Davis, was still more tied down. After all, the states which had formed the Confederacy had done so largely in order to protect states' rights. They were not willing to see those rights infringed, even by their own government, even to ensure their national survival.

The wartime increase in governmental power was, therefore, temporary. Lincoln was assassinated at the war's end and his Vice-President and successor, Andrew Johnson, became involved in a struggle for power with the Congressional leaders of the Republican Party. The occasion of the struggle was a dispute about the treatment of the conquered South, and especially about the conditions on which men from the Southern states should again be allowed to take their places in the Senate and the House of Representatives. Johnson favoured a lenient policy while the 'Radical Republicans', as they were called, favoured a more severe policy. Johnson was impeached and acquitted in the Senate by only a single vote — the only President to suffer the indignity of impeachment. Historians still differ about the implications of the struggle and about the motives of the contestants. For a time it looked as if the presidency might be brought under the control of the majority leaders in Congress. But it quickly became clear that, whoever controlled the federal government, its activities were not to be enlarged. There may have been a few among the Congressional leaders who were 'radical' in the sense that they wanted to make sweeping changes in society, and wanted to use the government to make them. There were not enough such radicals. For a few years they could use Northern resentment and fear of the South to win support; they could not do it for long. They lost support when it began to appear that changing the South would mean changing the North as well. Johnson was succeeded as President by General Grant, who held office from 1869 to 1877. Grant had been the most important and successful of the Northern commanders, but he was an inept and complacent politician, content as President to wait for instructions from Congress. Congress offered no effective leadership. Its members came to accept that there was nothing that the people wanted done.

The nation, therefore, resumed its growth after the

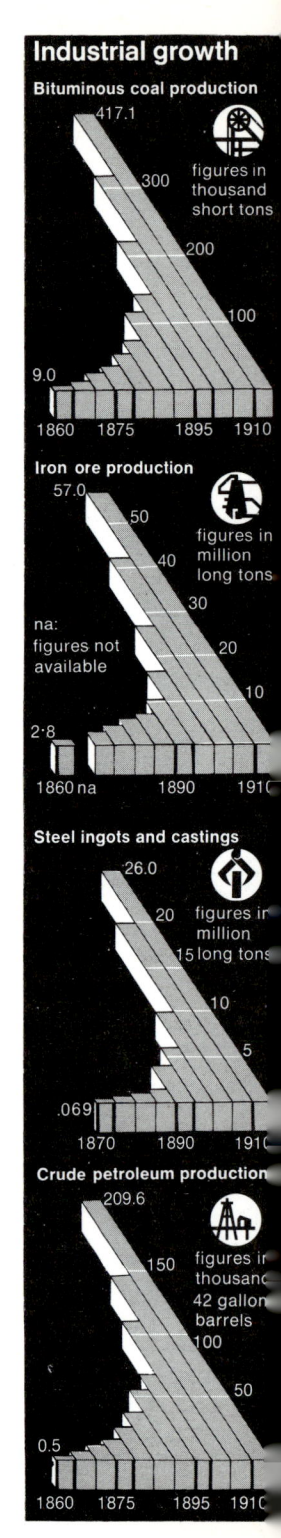

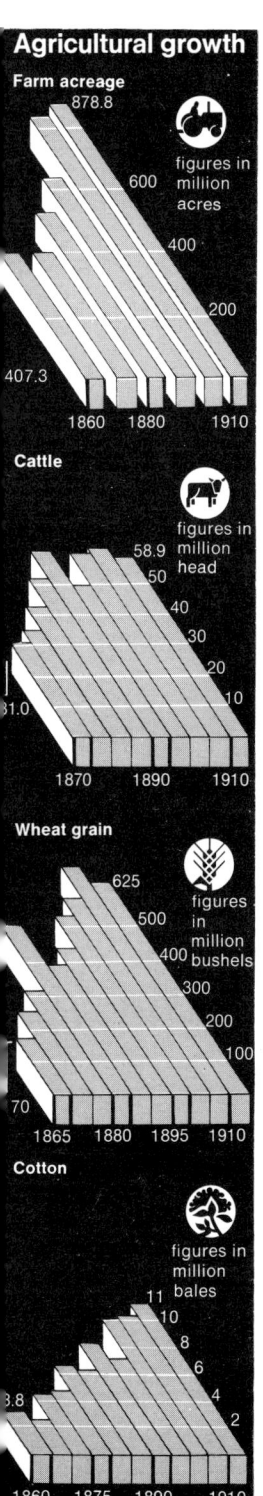

Civil War under the same weak government as before. Perhaps it would be more accurate to say that it continued its growth—at least in the North and West. Even before the war, the South had been falling behind the rest of the country in wealth and population. The war showed how great the Southern disadvantage was and may have preserved that disadvantage for two generations. The North boomed during the war; the South was almost ruined. Recovery for the South was a slow and painful business; the North was more prosperous when it made peace than it had been when it went to war. Though forced back into the Union, the South withdrew into a sort of isolation to wrestle with its two intertwined and intractable problems of race and poverty. The rest of the nation advanced. Northern prosperity had political consequences. Almost all classes and sections shared in it and it continued for almost a decade. Americans were confirmed in their support for their old institutions, and in their belief that the Civil War did not require them to make fundamental changes.

The bridge of steel

The most immediately obvious aspect of growth was expansion across the continent. Even before the Civil War the Pacific coast was being settled. California gained admission as a state in 1850, and Oregon, to the north, in 1859. Meanwhile, settlement to the east and west of the upper Mississippi established the states of Iowa (1846), Wisconsin (1848), and Minnesota (1858). Between these states and the Pacific Ocean, as down the whole country from north to south, stretched a vast region of almost empty national territory. Railways were obviously desirable to link the Pacific coast with the rest of the nation. Long before the war a line had been proposed and much discussed. The proposal had foundered on sectional differences over where the line should run. At that time, only a single route was in question. Most men supposed that there would not be sufficient traffic for more than one trans-continental line, but whatever the more distant future the first line would bring immediate advantages to the section from which it started. Northerners were not willing to see the line take a Southern route, which was at that time the cheapest and most obvious; Southerners were equally unwilling to concede a Northern route.

The outbreak of war settled the matter. President Lincoln chartered the first line in accordance with Northern interests during the war, and construction began shortly after its end. This was a departure which was to prove

Left: After the Civil War—the American 'economic miracle'

a precedent – a nationally-chartered line. If the line would serve a national purpose by linking East and West, it would also serve another purpose by making settlement possible in the country through which it ran. The expectation of development once the railway was built determined the conditions of its building. The line would be a private venture, privately built and privately run. The idea of a publicly-owned, or publicly-operated, railway was barely considered. Yet it was clear that initially traffic on the line would not be great enough to enable it to pay for its construction and use. The contractors therefore needed a subsidy. They were granted a subsidy in cash towards construction costs, but their most important subsidy was in land. Apart from the land actually needed for the railway lines, they were granted alternate sections of land in a checker-board pattern on either side of their track. This land they were entitled to sell when the existence of the railway tempted would-be settlers to buy it. The government retained control of the sections of land interspersed between those granted to the railway to ensure that, as land values rose, part of the added value would be retained for the public.

This manner of financing railway building followed naturally on an earlier decision. Land, unsettled and publicly-owned, had long been the chief national asset. There were two opinions as to how it should be used. One school thought that it should be sold at commercial prices. The income could be used for a whole range of useful national purposes, from reducing taxation to building roads, canals, dams, and harbours, or subsidising education. At various times some land was set aside for sale for specific purposes such as these. But in general the idea that public land should be a source of government revenue was rejected. Its unpopularity was on social rather than on economic grounds. It was undemocratic, for it confined the chance of winning land, and so of winning independence, to the rich. It was finally defeated with the passage of the Homestead Act in 1862, which made land in the national territories available very cheaply – in certain circumstances freely – to genuine settlers. That decision accorded with the whole ethos of an expansive people and an expanding nation. Once it had been taken, the decision to push railways across the country, in advance of settlement, followed naturally.

The first trans-continental line was built westwards by the Union Pacific Company, starting from Omaha on the Missouri River, until it met the line of the **26** ▷

Right: Casting pig iron in a Chicago iron and steel works. In the East and Middle West a giant industrial structure arose.
Next page: Meat packaging in a Cincinnati factory, 1890

Central Pacific Company, building eastwards from California. The building of such a line was a major feat both of engineering and of organisation. The builders had to drive a line with acceptable gradients through both the Sierra Nevada and the Rocky Mountain ranges, they had to work in conditions ranging from desert heat to mountain blizzards, and they had to keep labour gangs of thousands of men fed and supplied in uninhabited country. The Union Pacific relied on ex-servicemen and Irish immigrants to build the line. The Central Pacific used Irishmen too, but also imported large gangs of Chinese coolies. In actually laying the track the Irish were supreme – to manhandle the heavy sections of track into place called for great strength – but the willing endurance of the Chinese in all but the heaviest work was equally valuable. Building began slowly in 1864, but from 1867, when both companies were building in national territory, it turned into a race under the spur of a larger federal bounty to the company laying more track. The lines finally met at Promontory Point, Utah, in 1869 (the Union Pacific was judged to have won the race).

This line was, in any economic sense, a premature venture. It was built only because the government subsidised it. The government retained certain privileges, chief among them the right to move troops and government property by rail at much reduced rates, which, over the years, probably gave it an excellent return on its contribution. But the chief reason for government participation was simply the desire to unify and develop the nation. The terms on which the railway was built involved a sheer guess as to how quickly settlement would follow, and not much more than a guess as to how much it would cost to build. The land grant initially offered had to be doubled before anyone would undertake the venture. At first it was supposed that there could not be enough traffic for more than one transcontinental line. But so narrow a view was soon followed by over-optimism. The Northern Pacific was chartered in 1864, with a land grant but no construction loan, to run from the head of Lake Superior across the Northwest. Rather later, James J. Hill, one of the ablest of American railwaymen, constructed a second northern line, the Great Northern, the only system to be built without government subsidy. The construction of lines across the Southwest was a more complex and painful process, but finally two southern systems were put together: the Texas and Pacific, and the Atcheson, Topeka and Santa Fe. Once they were built, the size of the government subsidies and of the profits made by the companies became a source of political dispute.

The major railways were enterprises on a scale hitherto

unknown. By 1882, the Pennsylvania Railroad, one of the old-established eastern lines, was the largest private business in the world. It had 30,000 employees — far more than the federal government. Railways were highly technical enterprises, requiring skilled professional management. The railway companies were among the first to set up training schemes. The railwayman entered on his career for life. He abandoned, obviously, the prospect of setting up for himself, he did not move over to some other industry, indeed he usually stayed with one company. At the same time, railway development required larger amounts of capital than before. Railway finance followed a more erratic course than railway management, but in the course of their activities, and not least in the course of their struggles with each other, the railway magnates bought and sold large quantities of railway stock. Railways for long provided the largest part of the stock traded on American exchanges, and the existence of railways, with their financial needs and their financial vicissitudes, did much to build up the American stock market. Railways had another effect, not fully foreseen when the building boom began. They had often a good deal of choice as to where they would run across empty land. Their routes depended on engineering necessity, of course, but they were not so closely determined as those of rivers and canals. The railwaymen had power over the fate of local communities; they could make them prosperous by encouragement, or ruin them by neglecting or bypassing them. Railways were an invitation to pressure and counter-pressure of every political kind as an ordinary technique of business.

Impact of the railways
Exactly how important railways were in the growth of America is difficult to determine. Their influence mingled with many others and cannot be isolated. Growth remained a product of private enterprise. Had enterprise been denied outlet in railways, we may suppose that it would have found some other outlet. Yet railways, through both their building and their management, did provide one of the great outlets for enterprise, if not the greatest, in the thirty or forty years after the Civil War. Between 1870 and 1900 the mileage of American railway track almost quadrupled. It continued to increase till the 1920s, when the United States had more track than the whole of Europe. Railways were large users of iron and steel for track, rolling stock, and equipment. Before the Civil War the American iron and steel industry had languished under competition from Britain. Afterwards it

Left: Immigrants from Europe came to swell the labour force

27

was protected and began to grow. The huge iron ore deposits of Lake Superior were developed and the ore transported by water to refining centres like Chicago and Milwaukee. Some ore went to Pittsburgh itself, the centre of the Pennsylvania coal field. The railways increasingly linked the United States into a single great market. Those who produced efficient or desirable goods could sell them all over the country, as the transport element in costs was reduced. Perhaps most important of all, though impossible to measure, is the impact of railways on the American imagination. They symbolized the assurance of future growth, and so sustained the optimism and the readiness to gamble which are essential to the growth of an uncontrolled economy.

Confidence in growth was, as we shall see, sometimes exaggerated and sometimes misplaced; but it was sufficiently justified to continue. Fundamentally it rested on the abundance of American natural resources. These were years in which it seemed that the country could meet any demand made of it. In agriculture, in mining, in manufacturing, it was a poor index that could only double between 1870 and 1900. A key index like that for the production of pig iron showed an eightfold increase.

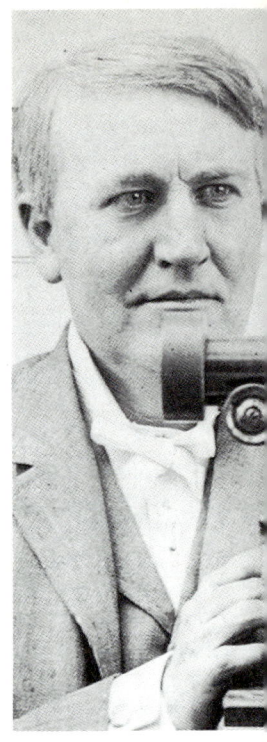

New Americans

None of this growth would have been possible without an adequate supply of labour. That also was available, for the immigrants continued to come, and in increasing numbers. Immigration from Europe fluctuated widely from year to year, for various reasons, some European and some American, but after 1865 it never fell below 100,000. It rose as high as 974,000 in 1905, with an intermediate peak of 648,000 in 1882. Increasingly the immigrants came from the southern and eastern regions of Europe. The British, the Irish, the Germans, and the Scandinavians continued to come, but their numbers remained fairly steady or began to fall away. They were now supplemented by Poles, Hungarians, Italians, and East European Jews. These began to arrive from the ending of the Civil War onwards, though the tide swelled to a flood only after the beginning of the 20th century. In 1905, the peak year, 185,000 immigrants came from Russia, 221,000 from Italy, and 276,000 from Austria-Hungary. This flood of new immigrants helped to ensure the growth of American population, and with it of American output, at a pace which no European state could match.

With immigrants and industry and improved transport came, inevitably, the growth of American cities. In 1860 only 20 per cent of the American population was described by the census as urban. By 1900 the figure was 40 per cent. Though in the census any place with a

population of more than 2,500 was classed as urban, the move to the cities and the growth of the cities was indisputable. Increasingly the problems of cities, rather than their advantages, caught the attention. Immigrants were not responsible for these problems, though they shared in them and perhaps intensified some of them. Native Americans were also moving away from the land. Whatever the problems of the cities they were created by Americans. The cities grew because Americans moved into them in preference to staying where they were. It is as true of city problems as of other problems in this period that they were the reverse side of American advantages.

This point can be made general, and it offers perhaps the best clue through the labyrinth of American history in the period between the Civil War and the First World War. The basic American advantage was abundance; but the basic American problem was over-abundance. So far we have been dealing with the growth of the American economy. Equally noticeable was the fact that the size of the units in important industries was growing, with the formation of gigantic 'trusts', so that there seemed real danger of monopoly. Various factors were at work and every industry calls for its own analysis. Perhaps most important, however, was the desire of businessmen to control supplies and markets. The danger which they wanted to avert was that overproduction would force prices down to ruinous levels. Some industries lent themselves to control more easily than others. The most notorious of the business trusts, that of Standard Oil, came about because a businessman of unusual ruthlessness and clear-sightedness, John D. Rockefeller, grasped the fact that by controlling oil-refining he could control both the numerous producers and the numerous retailers of oil. In some other industries patents could be used to sustain a monopoly. More typically, however, in a society dedicated to competition, the actual merging of rival firms was the only means by which a market could be controlled. Many American difficulties, practical and ideological, derived from the fact that some parts of the economy were more readily controlled than others, and that businessmen devised means of control for their purposes before other groups did for theirs. In particular, farmers and workingmen found it very difficult to limit or control the supply of what they had to offer. To some of the difficulties which that caused we can now turn.

Left: Titans of the economy: inventor Thomas Edison **(top left)**; banker J.P.Morgan **(top right)**; industrialist Andrew Carnegie **(bottom left)**; press tycoon William R.Hearst **(bottom right)**

Chapter 2
The Cost of Expansion

Though American growth continued after the Civil War with no less speed and vitality than before, it did not take place at an equal rate everywhere. The United States was, and is, a country of great diversity – huge, sprawling, containing extremes of climate and wide variations of natural resources. As the railways opened up the country, these variations became even more apparent, and made an even greater effect on politics than had been the case when settlement was concentrated to the east of the Mississippi. If their country had been poor, Americans would have had to endure poverty. Because it was rich and they knew it to be rich, they began to complain when they were denied a share in its ever-growing wealth. But because the country was so various, and because the pattern of settlement constantly changed, politics could never become a simple struggle between rich and poor. Though discontent was always there, it was often too local, or too specific, or too short-lived to win redress. Moreover, and more immediately important, the Civil War itself had caused dislocation which was to affect national politics for two generations and which made it more difficult to come to grips with other problems.

The effect of the Civil War was most noticeable in the South. The Confederacy had fought against a superior opponent with an effectiveness which still surprises historians, but final victory was beyond its resources. For some years Northern politicians feared or pretended to fear that the South might renew its treachery, but to any discerning eye it quickly became apparent that the South had been almost ruined by the war. Even before the war, though Southern agriculture was efficient, and though most historians believe that slavery was profitable, the South was falling behind the rest of the nation in economic growth, and especially in industrialisation. Increasingly – as Southerners knew and Southerners resented – the South was a supplier of raw materials to the rest of the nation and the rest of the world. After the war it was hard to break out of that position. The

Left: *The dark side of industrialisation – a juvenile mill-hand*

31

freeing of the slaves had destroyed a great deal of Southern capital at a single blow and, in contrast to British practice when slavery was abolished in the West Indies, the slave owners had not been compensated. Neither had the slaves. The South was a land where labour was plentiful but where profitable outlets and capital to create them were lacking. In the circumstances, the region was largely thrown back on what it had been doing already and what it knew how to do—the growing of cotton.

Even in cotton growing the shortage of capital did much to determine organisation. Those who could by any means lay their hands on some capital advanced it to the small growers who needed tools, a mule, seed, and something to live on while waiting for the crop. They often lent them the land as well. In return the capitalists received a share of the crop—the 'share cropping' system was born. It was a system which, once developed, would have been exceedingly difficult to break in any circumstances. If the production of cotton had been profitable the creditor would have been in a strong position and reluctant to see his debtors break free; and since he controlled the marketing of the crop they would have found it hard to turn to new sources of credit. In fact, it was not profitable. Cotton was no longer king. During the Civil War, largely in response to the world shortage of cotton which the war created, new sources of supply had been discovered and their development continued after the war. The Southern cotton growers were working in a world which often had an oversupply of cotton, but their dependence on cotton continued. Creditors and debtors alike were impoverished, and caught in the same trap—the creditors had no alternative but to continue staking their debtors in an unprofitable activity.

It would be wrong to picture the state of the South as uniformly bleak. Change and development were under way even there. Northern capitalists had no objection in principle to investing in the South when opportunity offered. There was a certain amount of industrialisation. Cotton goods manufacturing began to move south. An iron and steel industry was developed in the region around Birmingham, Alabama. Trade began to revive and New Orleans especially remained a major port. But the generalisation stands. By and large, men with capital in the years following the Civil War found better outlets for it than the South, and the South in consequence remained relatively depressed. Some historians have recently argued that if the freed Negro slaves had been given land and some equipment with which to work it—forty acres and a mule, in the phrase of the time—they would have

Right: Beauty in squalor—George Bellow's 'Lone Tenement'

gained economic independence and so have laid earlier the only sound basis for that real political independence which they have still to win. It is hard to see how this theory can be sustained. The basic problem, after all, was over-production of cotton in a world market—and agricultural over-production brings debt and tenancy with it the world over.

Nor did diversification offer a way out. One may reasonably ask why, if too much cotton was being grown, Southern farmers did not produce something else. Part of the answer is simply that cotton was what they knew how to produce, and it was hard to shake the faith, developed over many years, that there would always be a demand for it. Another reason is that the share cropping system had men in its grip. But yet another is that the alternatives to cotton were not promising either. As the railway system developed, the first thing it did was to open up new farming land. Initially at least the new land was often more fertile than the old, and at first it could be had very cheaply. As men moved on to new regions and opened them up, the general effect was to induce over-production of almost every farm product. That this was the problem was not usually apparent at once. With a growing population, the demand for food, and for more varieties of food, was growing; but it did not keep pace with the supply. Emigration from the South to more fertile and prosperous regions was not very great; but had it been greater, it is unlikely that many of those who moved would have benefited themselves much.

The story of American farming in the later 19th century is complicated. The hope of independence and fortune lured many on to lands which were not really suitable for exploitation. The climate in the West was too harsh, especially in dry years, though the yields of early crops on new soil concealed the fact for a time. The farmers who suffered most were those producing a staple crop, especially grain. Because their market was not only nationwide but worldwide, the price of their crops was determined by a world price which they could not influence, while their expenses too were matters over which they had no control. Neither increased production, which only made things worse, nor self-restraint in keeping production down, which made things no better, could help them. Rigid conservatism was not the problem. American farmers were not peasants. They were not stubbornly wedded to old ways of doing things when better ways offered. They were not even stubbornly attached to one piece of land rather than to another. They

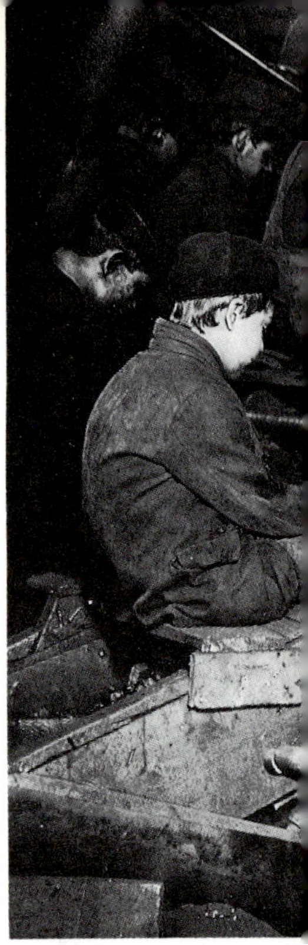

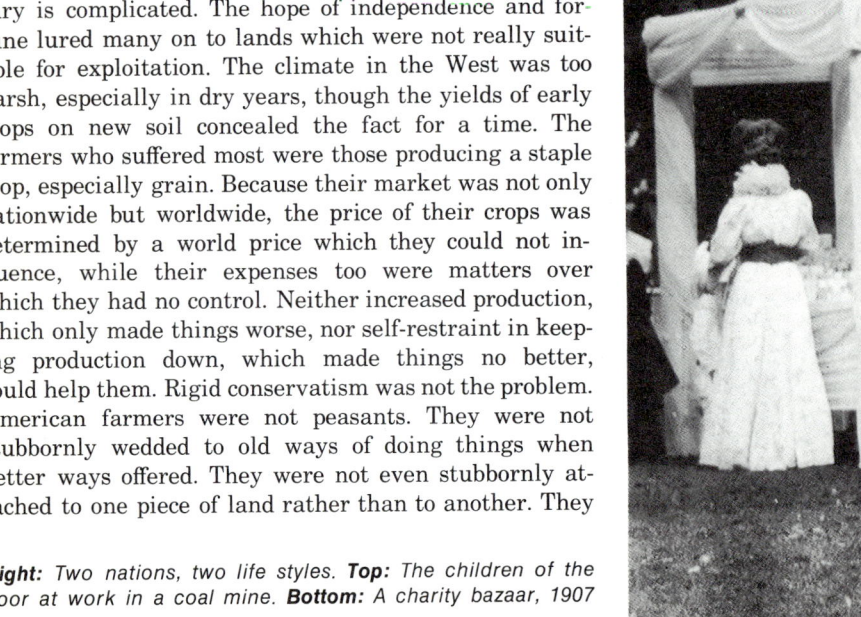

Right: Two nations, two life styles. **Top:** The children of the poor at work in a coal mine. **Bottom:** A charity bazaar, 1907

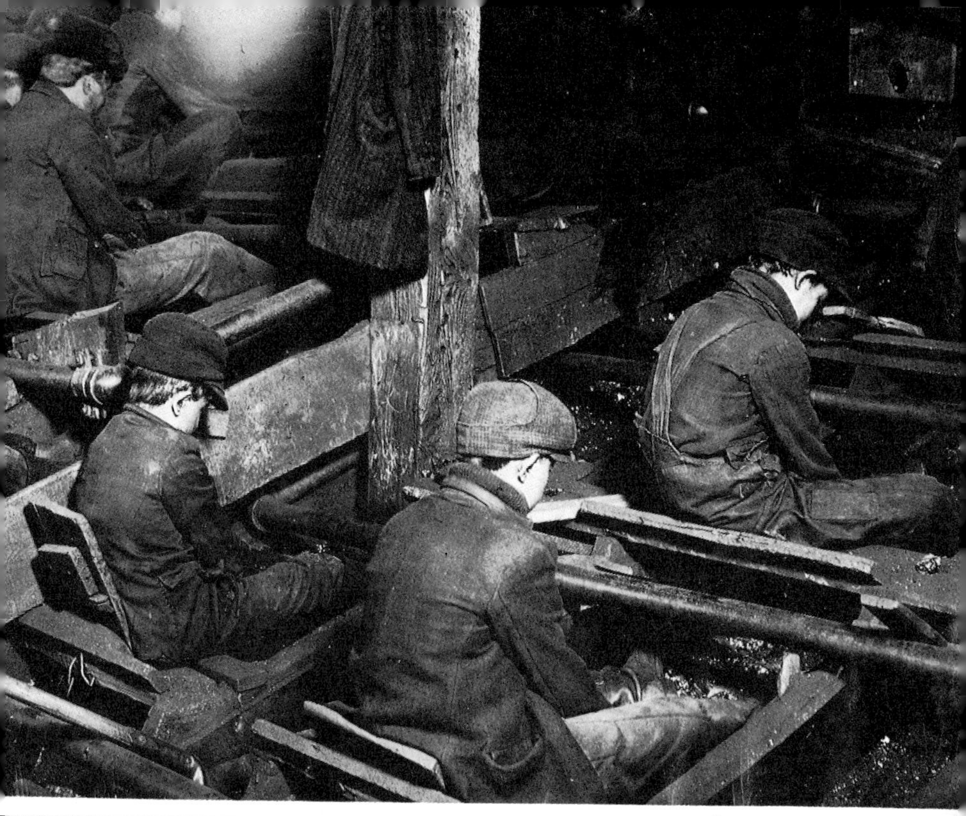

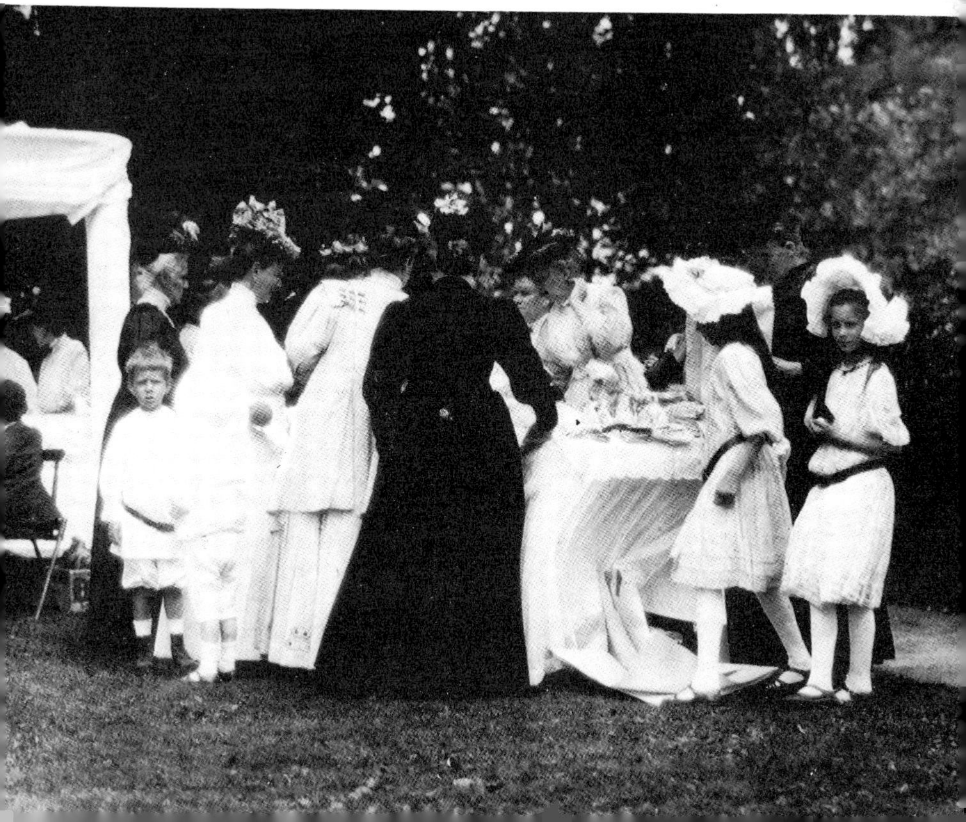

were adaptable, and within limits mobile. It is noticeable that as the country opened up, the centres of farm discontent moved west with settlement.

For this various reasons have been advanced. Some have suggested that the most restless and rootless farmers were the most likely to be discontented. More precisely and plausibly it has been pointed out that as settlement developed, so did cities, and cities provided farmers with the opportunity for new kinds of farming—dairy, vegetable, and fruit farming, and the supply of fresh meat—which were all more profitable than the basic grain farming to which farmers had been confined before and which now moved further west onto still newer land. The patterns of farm discontent, its geographical movements, and its rise and fall between good times and bad, have yet to be fully analysed. But exactly what farmers complained about has been thoroughly established. They complained about interest rates. Inevitably they said that they had to pay too much to borrow money, and that money-lenders were making excessive profits. Against such sharp practice, farmers thought they were entitled to government protection. In the end, many came round to demanding simply that the government itself should lend them money at 'reasonable' rates against the security of their crops. Initially, however, they had a simpler remedy. The reason for high interest rates, they argued, was a shortage of money—as with any commodity, when money was scarce one had to pay more for it. The government controlled the money supply. It should, therefore, issue more, thus automatically bringing interest rates down. This adherence to the 'quantity theory' of money, in its simplest form, was a recurring grievance, which ran through the farm regions whenever times were bad.

Other farmers' complaints were more specific. They complained that they had to sell always at the same time, when prices were low, while the benefit of rising prices at other times of the year went to the owners of grain elevators. They complained about railway freight rates, claiming both that they were too high and that they were not equitably fixed. They complained that when tenants improved their farms the benefit went not to them but to their landlords. Such complaints tipped easily into the belief that landowners, railway owners, and grain elevator owners had corrupted the legislators so that farmers could gain no legislative redress. Though their difficulties were real and must win sympathy, farmers were too ready to suspect a conspiracy against them. Their basic difficulty was that they were trying to sell in a world market which was suffering from a glut of farm produce, and that the orthodox economic theory of the day precluded much

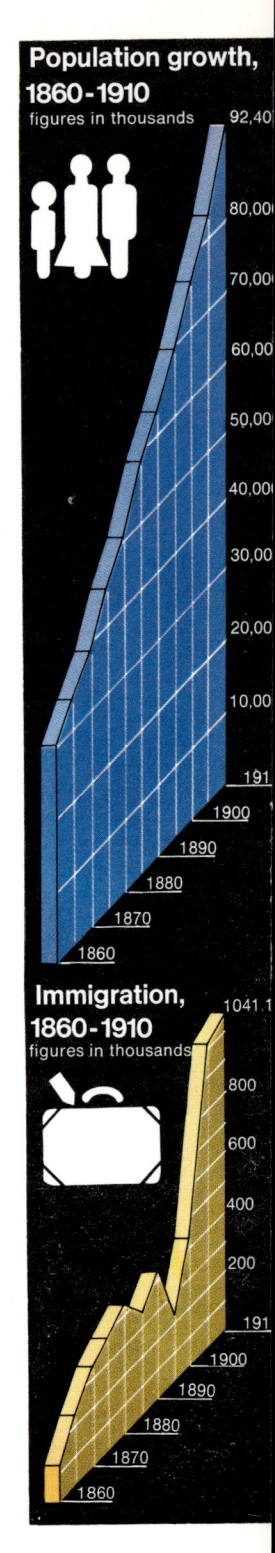

Immigration
By country of origin
1860 / 1910

- 1.6 / —
- 2.9 / —
- 3.6 / — All other countries 5.4%
- 4.2 / 0.7 Canada and Newfoundland 5.4%
- — / 0.2% China
- — / Other European countries
- — / 20.7% Italy
- 35.4 / 0.5
- — / Russia (European) 20.7%
- 31.7 / Austria-Hungary 24.9%
- — / 3.0% Germany
- — / Scandinavia 4.6%
- — / 2.9% Ireland
- 19.4 / Great Britain 6.5%

government help.

The farmers' complaints, which grew louder as the century wore to its end, were those of men engaged in a traditional activity. But although these were years in which more new land was brought under cultivation than in the entire earlier history of the United States, they were also an era in which the balance of population was swinging against the countryside. More and more Americans were moving into and living in towns. It was urban America which was expanding most rapidly. In this fact, indeed, lay the ultimate salvation of those farmers who stayed on the land and knew how to adapt, for it was the business of supplying food to towns which kept them going. But as the towns expanded, they brought new problems, or problems which, if not new, were at least new in scale. The problems were those of congestion, of industrial relations, and sometimes of relations among immigrant groups of different origins. Like the problems of all modern cities, they derived from the growth of industry and the development of transport. Like the problems of Western farmers, they were the price paid for growth and could hardly have been avoided. But, like the problems of Southern farmers, they were intensified by the Civil War. The war gave an artificial stimulus to American industry, an unbridled quality to its expansion, and unusual opportunities to the unscrupulous. Prudence and honesty were both hard to find in the post-war years, and so was social concern.

The robber barons

It is remarkable how many of the great American fortunes had their origin in the Civil War. There had been earlier fortunes. When John Jacob Astor died in 1848, that poor German immigrant left the unheard-of sum of twenty million dollars. 'Commodore' Cornelius Vanderbilt, who survived to become one of the most colourful and thrusting buccaneers of the post-war years, had built a large shipping fortune well before the war. But men like Jay Gould, John Pierpont Morgan, Philip Armour, Andrew Carnegie, James J.Hill, John D.Rockefeller—the household names of the later 19th century—were all in their early twenties when the war broke out. Huntington and Stanford, the West Coast railway kings, were just over thirty. Jay Cooke, the banker who did more than anyone to finance the Northern war effort, and whose spectacular failure some years later was the direct cause of the crash of 1873, was not yet forty. These were not men who served in the war. Most of them got their start by supplying the armies. The war taught two les-

Left: A growing population—and a changing ethnic balance

sons which enterprising men were quick to learn. If politicians could help one to win contracts on profitable terms, that help was worth paying for. And, when prices responded sharply to the changing fortunes of war, good information and rapid decisions made money. As Daniel Drew, one of the early railway magnates, put it: 'It's good fishing in troubled waters.' Philip Armour, founder of one of the great meat-packing firms, was early in the business of supplying salt pork to the Union armies. In 1865 he contracted to supply large quantities, which he did not have, at the rate of forty dollars a barrel. As he had foreseen, the price of pork collapsed after the Confederate General Lee's surrender at Appomattox. Buying enough to meet his contract at eighteen dollars a barrel, he made a rapid profit of two million dollars.

Armour's coup, if morally dubious, was legally impeccable. His profit was the reward of sound judgment, boldly backed. Some activities were of a different order. The directors of the Union Pacific Railroad set up a construction company, grandly styled the Crédit Mobilier. By awarding the company absurdly profitable construction contracts, they brought the Union Pacific to the edge of bankruptcy while diverting twenty million dollars of public money into their own pockets. In the hope of averting a Congressional investigation, the directors placed blocks of Crédit Mobilier stock 'where they would do most good'. When the scandal broke, during the election campaign of 1872, it ended the careers of several prominent politicians, headed by the Vice-President, Schuyler Colfax, but, revealingly enough, no criminal charges were brought. In a scandal like that of the Crédit Mobilier politicians rather than businessmen suffered most from the evidence of corruption. It was, after all, the duty of elected representatives to resist attempts to bribe them. The demand for reform, which first gathered strength after the war, was a demand for the reform of government, as the corruption which flourished under President Grant's easy-going sway became offensively open. One of the most damaging charges against the governments imposed by the North on the defeated Southern states was that they were corrupt. Recent historians have done something to defend the post-war Southern legislatures, chiefly by arguing that, so far as they were corrupt, they only shared a corruption which was equally widespread, and far more ingenious and expensive, in the North itself.

Danger for the small businessman
Corruption continued to be a problem in local government, especially perhaps in transport, in which the links between private enterprise and government must be close, though even here operators needed more help from politi-

cians when they were building their lines than later when they were running them. In manufacturing, any danger from corruption soon became secondary to the mere fact that some firms were large and powerful and rich enough to prevent the success of their rivals. It began to look as if the small man would lose his chance of ever getting a start in business, or at any rate in the most lucrative sorts of business. A few large companies dominated many industries – textile machinery, agricultural machinery, barbed wire, meat packing, and many others. The advantage of those who had happened to get there first, often by being in the right place during the Civil War, seemed impossible to overcome.

It is important to be clear what the ground of complaint against big business was. The rise of the trust, even the growth of monopoly, did not, with occasional exceptions, directly damage Americans as consumers. These companies did not threaten the American standard of living; they threatened the American way of life. Big business was, of course, not new, nor has business ceased to grow since that time; to some people today huge industrial concerns once again seem to be a threat to democracy. But the danger in late 19th-century America was different. Even the largest corporations were usually personally owned. It was the *owners* of great corporations, not the mere managers who have succeeded them, who seemed to constitute the threat. A few men of ever-growing wealth seemed likely to engross the resources of the country, and so to deny others any hope of a share. One aspect of late 19th-century industry is relevant and important here. Men knew that they were experiencing an industrial revolution, but they lacked the modern sense, born of ever more rapid scientific invention, that the revolution would continue for ever and that no one could foresee its course. In particular, they thought it was a revolution in power, in metals, and in transport. Those who controlled the supplies of those vital basic industrial ingredients could hold their countrymen to ransom. The huge oil trust of Standard Oil, put together by Rockefeller, or United States Steel, put together by J.P.Morgan on the basis of Carnegie's empire, seemed to block for ever the hope of similar exploits, and with that hope went an important part of the American dream. For that reason above all, the men who owned American industry seemed frighteningly powerful, the more so at a time when the institutions of government were weak. There seemed little the government could do to limit either the wealth   42 ▷

Left: The urban landscape – an industrial sector of Lynn, Massachusetts. **Next page, left:** A slum alley in New York's Lower East Side. **Right:** Hoffman House, a fashionable saloon

39

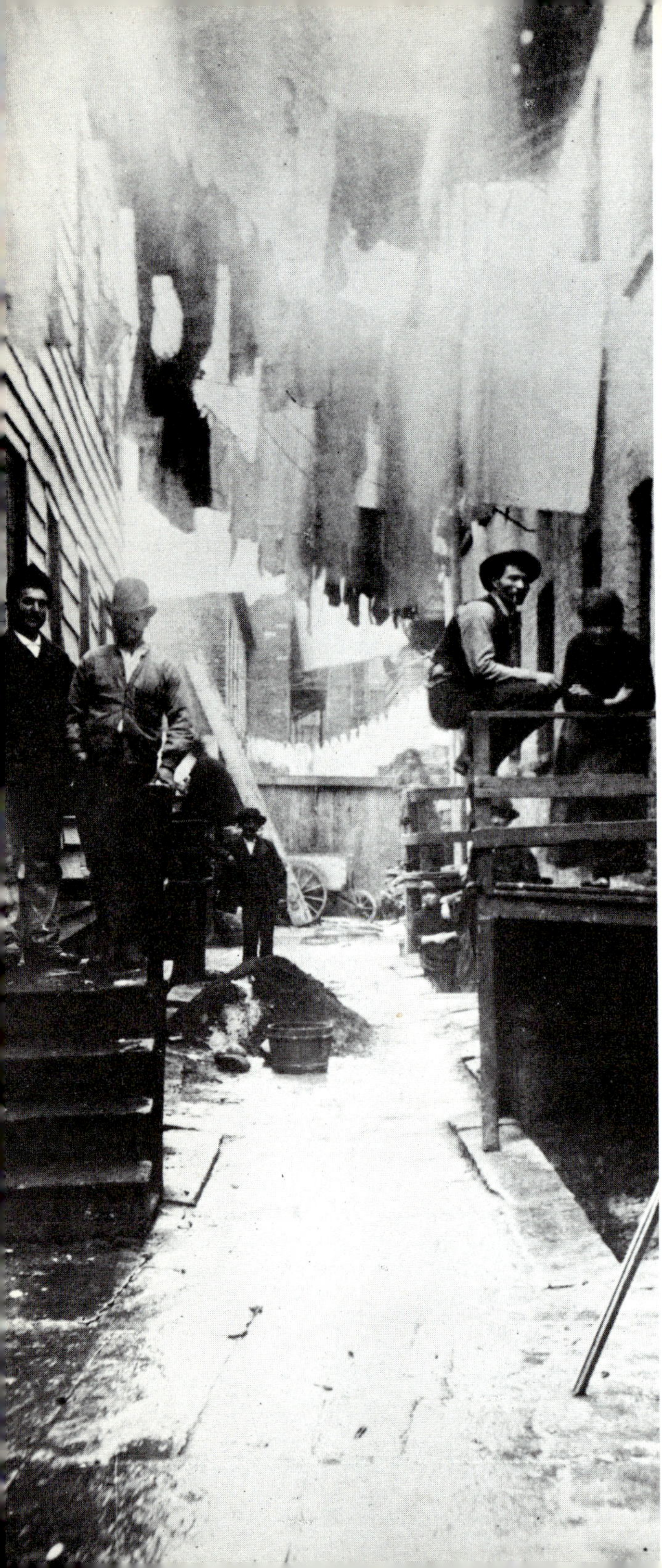
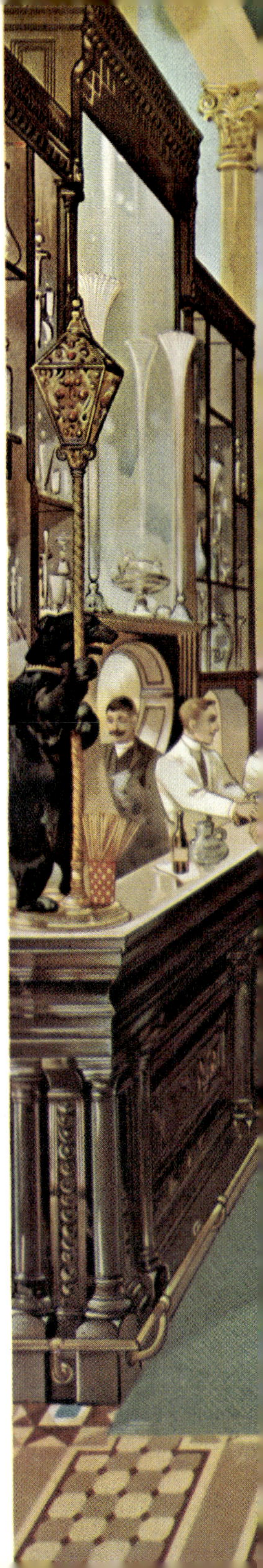

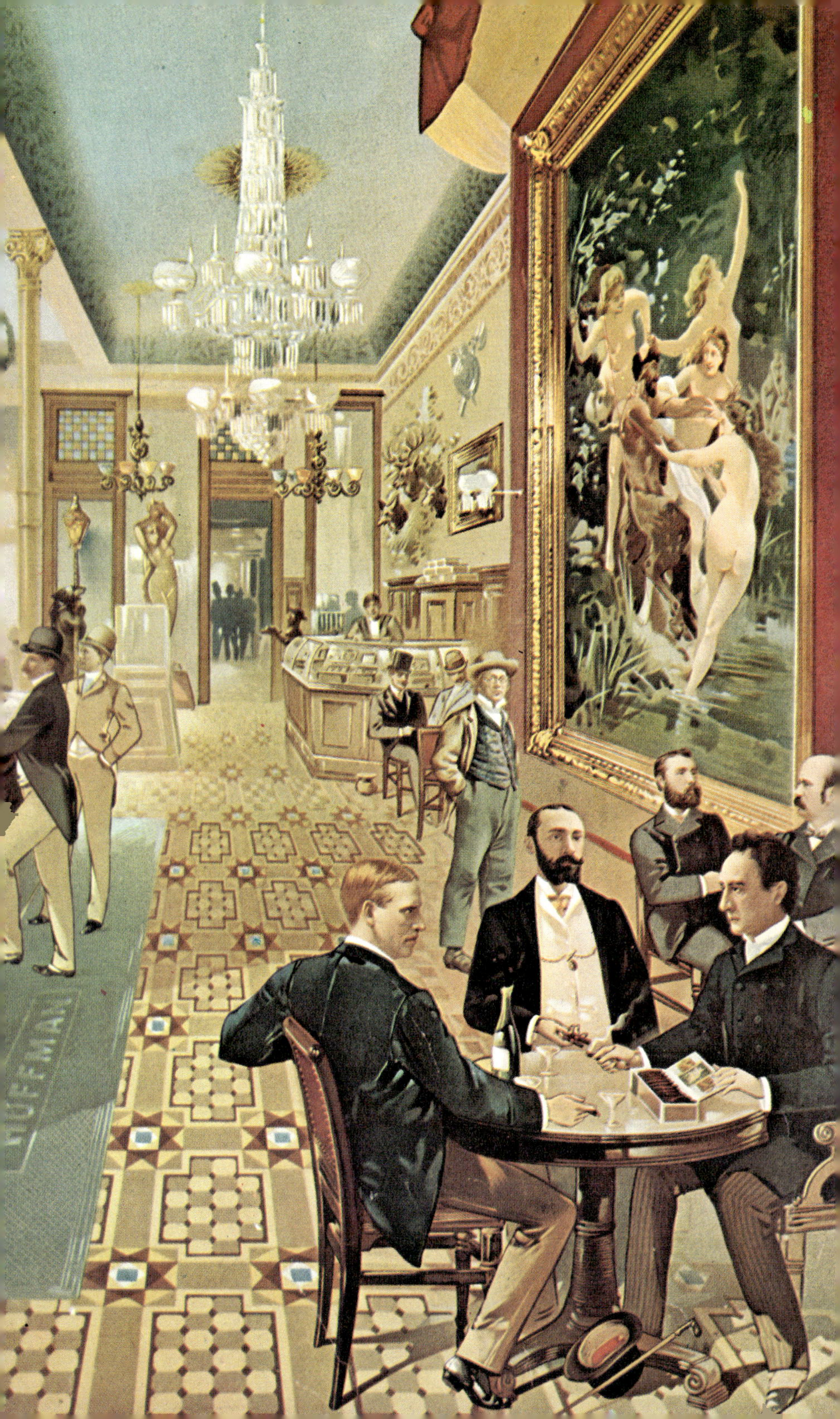

of the tycoons or the power it enabled them to wield.

If the problem of dealing with trusts became the most characteristic problem of the Progressive era, it was not the only one nor even, perhaps, the most difficult. Most American businesses remained comparatively small, but even these felt the strain of intensified competition, and even in these relations between employers and employees became thin and remote. The growth of modern society threatened and finally ended an old and very pervasive American dream—that the employee was only passing through a phase on the way to his own independence. Increasingly, it became clear that most Americans, for good or ill, would remain employees all their working lives, and with that realization came the development of the trade union movement. As earlier in Britain, the movement ran into heavy opposition on the ground that it infringed the right of the free worker to drive his own best bargain as an individual with his employer. Moreover, in the United States the tradition of free enterprise was stronger than in Europe and the tradition of government regulation was almost wholly lacking. Another element in opposition to unions was the belief among consumers that their success would increase prices. In this view, unions, like business trusts, were combinations in restraint of trade. It took time to establish the view that labour should not be treated as a mere commodity. The early union leaders had to fight not only against employers, but against a public opinion which was always liable to hostility. They may have benefited from public concern with the great corporations, as they did from the tendency of employers to exploit their advantages, thus incurring popular opposition, but they had to move with caution and their successes were hardly won.

Inevitably linked with the growth of industry was the growth of towns. While land transport remained horse-drawn, there was a limit to the size to which cities, other than ports, could grow. Rail transport made it possible to feed and supply much larger centres. But though cities *could* now grow, they did grow because they had positive advantages. Just as it was possible to feed larger conglomerations of people, so it was possible to carry away the manufactures of cities to serve a larger area. The inland American cities were, until recently, raw and lacking in much cultural life, but they were thriving centres of manufacture, and as industry boomed so did the commercial and financial services which it requires. Yet this story of growth had another side. The United States lacked a real urban tradition—the sort of civic pride

Right, top: Kentucky farm family—in rural areas too poverty was widespread. **Bottom:** But for some life was very pleasant

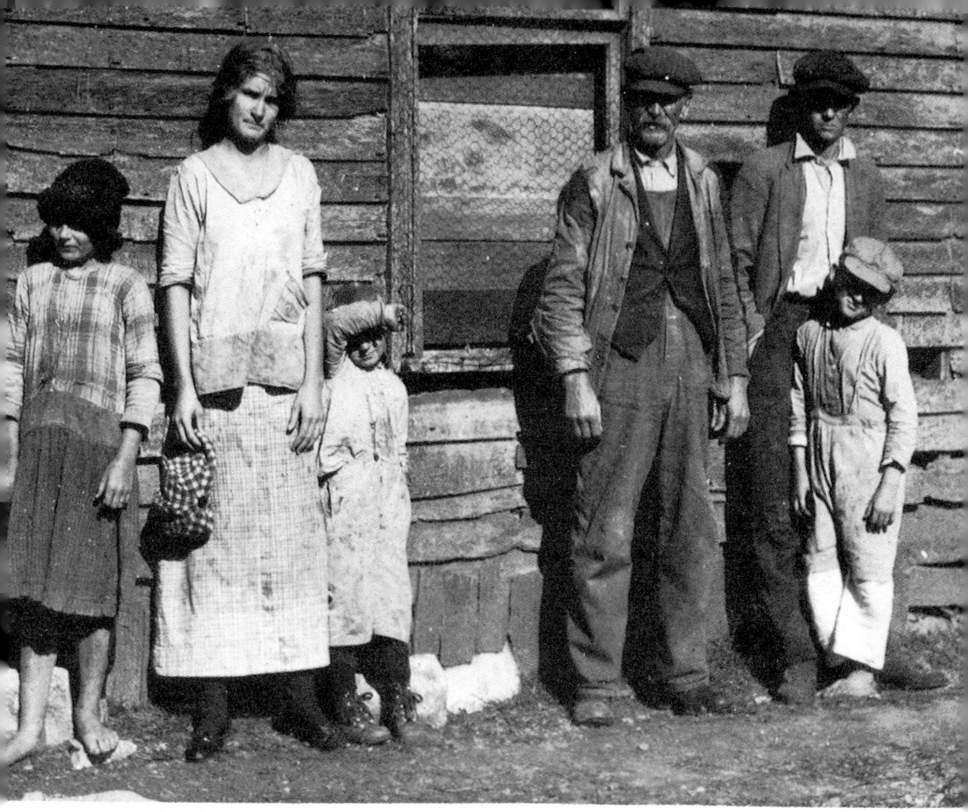

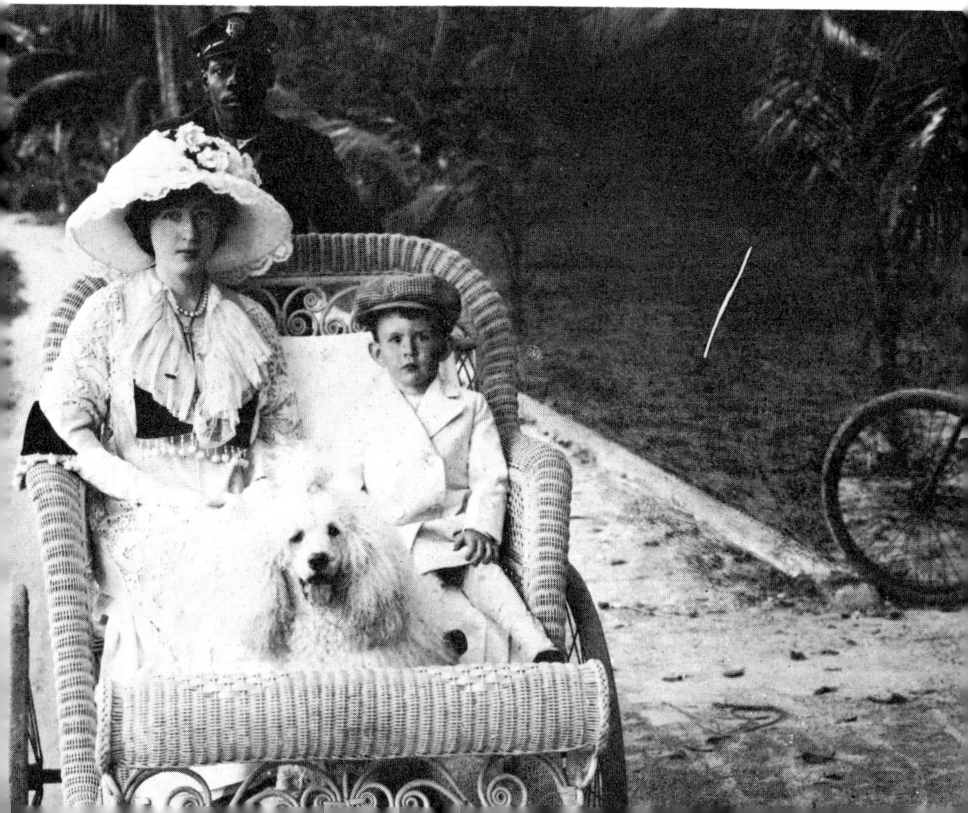

which many of the ancient towns of Europe had known and which had done something to make for efficient government. There was little tradition of effective local government outside New England, and even there it had weakened considerably. Nor was there much of a tradition of local leadership by leading families, for that would be an affront to egalitarianism. The towns of America grew haphazardly, and in this atmosphere the problems of housing, of sanitation, of local transport, of police, of services, proved intransigent.

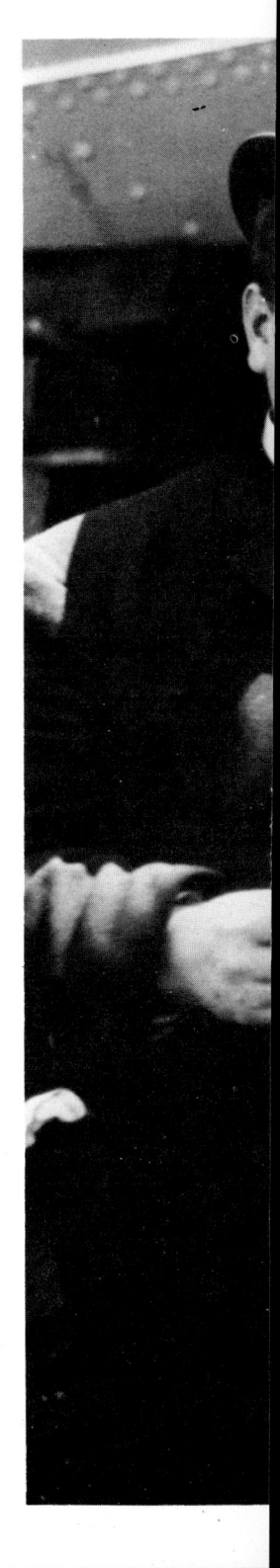

Struggling with these problems, and trying to adapt their own ideas and institutions, Americans were made conscious that, for some men at least, America was still the land of opportunity. The influx of immigrants continued but, as we have seen, increasingly they came from new parts of Europe. The reasons for this shift are more European than American. Improved transport and the relaxation of restrictions by their own governments made it possible for many Europeans to emigrate who would have been prevented earlier. At the same time, the development of Western European economies, the German for example, created opportunities at home for men who might earlier have been tempted overseas. There is little evidence that the new immigrants came for reasons different from those of the old. Some certainly came with the help of shipping firms who wanted to fill their ships, or of employers who wanted labour. Some certainly had at the back of their minds the idea of going home when they had made a stake—faster steamships also increased the amount of re-migration back across the Atlantic. But most immigrants came for traditional reasons. They wanted to become Americans. Because they came to a country which for them was frightening and strange they tended, as they had always done, to settle where there were others from their homeland who could console and instruct them in the ways of their new country. In an America of mushrooming towns, this created racial ghettoes. For Americans faced with all the problems which this chapter has attempted to sketch, it was all too easy to see immigrants as complicating if not actually causing these problems. The overcrowding and the slums could conveniently be attributed to dirty foreign habits. The difficulty of forming labour unions could be attributed to the readiness of foreign blacklegs to break strikes. Even the weakness of government and the difficulty of reform could be attributed to the lack of interest of these newcomers in democracy, their ignorance and docility and readiness to sell their votes to local bosses of their own race, who would in turn sell them to corrupt politicians. On the other side, foreigners brought with them strange and dangerous European doctrines, such as socialism and anarchism, which would undermine the fabric of America. Most historians would agree that this range of complaints against immigrants indicates not the real nature of the newcomers, but the discontents of Americans with their society and with evils which seemed too big to handle. Just for that reason it is worth emphasising, as remarkable and touching, how little racialism there was in America and how powerful the tradition of an open welcome to newcomers remained until after the First World War.

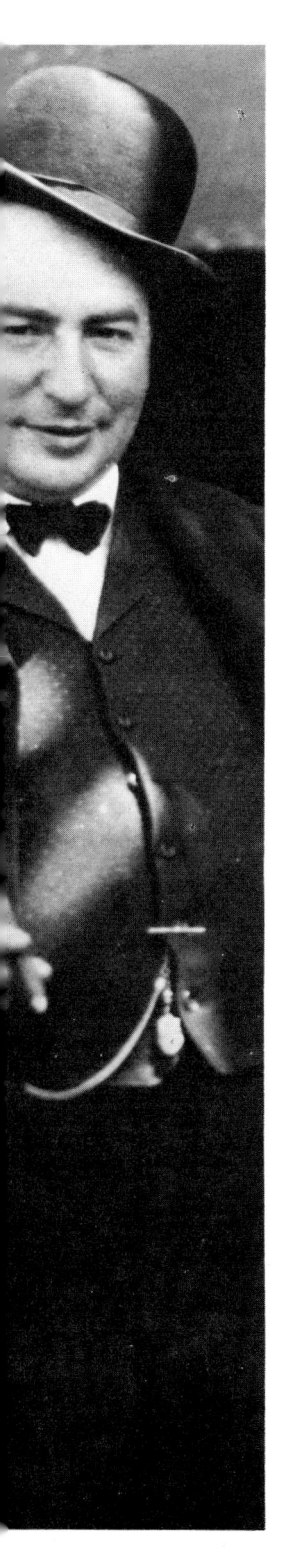

Among the discontented native American groups we must include the middle classes. Not all of them were discontented, of course, but a great many solid American citizens felt that the America they knew and understood — and in a real sense had controlled — was slipping away from them. They had little to complain of in a material sense, except perhaps that some Americans could realise a degree of ostentation hitherto unknown, but they were questioning and uneasy. Their discontent was probably more influential than any other element in bringing about change. Yet the roots of that discontent are not easy to uncover, for they ran in many directions. Here only two points need be made. First, for most Americans their problems were still domestic, little complicated by international concerns. Second, those of the middle classes who felt concern did not sink back into mindless conservatism or find easy scapegoats. Much as they differed among themselves they clung to certain shared virtues; and when they looked around for the men who threatened their virtues, they blamed tycoons rather than immigrants.

One distinctive group in American society which had every reason to be discontented could be, and was, neglected. In 1901, W.E.B.DuBois, the Negro historian, wrote: 'The problem of the 20th century is the problem of the color line.' But in the 19th century that problem could simply be ignored. The National Association for the Advancement of Colored People was founded only in 1910, significantly enough in the North and by a group of reformers who had experience of work with other minority groups in the cities. Even after it was founded it remained for some years small and not very effective. The great migration of Southern Negroes to the cities of the North, which has forced the problems of Negroes on the national attention, had not yet taken place. Because the South remained in many ways an area apart and an area for which the national government did not cater, the problems of the Negroes went almost unremarked as well as unredressed.

Left: Politician, St Louis style — indifferent and corrupt civil government was a persistent evil in American society

FOR SALE
TO LET
CLOSED
TO LET
FACTORY
CLOSED
FREE TRADER
ANARCHY
HARD TIMES.
BUSTED DINNER PAIL.

Chapter 3
Politicians and Reformers

The causes of discontent described in the previous chapter built up slowly after the Civil War. At first, outside the South, complacency was a more dominant emotion. The war was over and the victory had been won. If there was a national problem it was to ensure that the fruits of victory were not lost by carelessness in peacetime. The South must be prevented from renewing rebellion, and the country must be kept in safe hands – which meant the hands of the Republican Party. This was a powerful element, though not the only one, in Republican policy in the years just after the war. The attitude it exploited, however, could not last. Though the veterans of the war remained a powerful lobby, demanding and getting generous pensions, interest in the war and its memories began to fade as men turned to other pursuits. Danger from the South seemed less and less real. The wartime boom in the North continued for some years after the war was over, and even when depression struck in 1873 it did not last long enough seriously to shake the attitudes formed earlier.

If general complacency dictated governmental inaction, so did the nation's political structure. Neither of the major national parties was ordinarily a party of reform. The Democratic Party had once had a tradition of vigorous presidential leadership in the popular cause. But before the Civil War it had become increasingly Southern-dominated, and so committed to the doctrine that the Constitution limited the scope of the federal government. The following of the Republican Party, which had gained its first victory only with Lincoln in 1860, derived chiefly from the old Whig Party which, as the party of the prosperous and the respectable, had generally been cautious and conservative. Moreover, the strains that occurred against the general background of post-war prosperity were caused by differences between one region and another, or between one group and another. Political quarrels were about who should get

Left: *1908 anti-Bryan cartoon depicts the great politician with his reputed allies – socialism, 'hard times', anarchy*

47

BOYCOTT
MOB VIOLENCE
RIOT
INTIMIDATION
PERSUASION
ANARCHY
INCENDIARY PRESS
PARKISM
GRAFT
MITCHELL
UNIONISM

what; they were not yet quarrels about what the nature of American society should be. Old virtues were still thought adequate. Men who were unscrupulous in their personal dealings found it convenient to uphold the system, and men who were unfortunate blamed corruption rather than the system. Such conflict among sections or groups made effective action on a national level difficult. There was no national policy, there could be no national policy, because no group or coalition of groups was strong enough to capture the national government. Indeed, for considerable periods, none was even much interested in capturing it. To this period belongs James Bryce's classic description of the two major national parties as 'like two identical bottles, each labelled "empty"'.

The difficulties facing reformers can be shown in the history of the first post-war reform movement. The struggle following Lincoln's death between President Johnson and Congress has already been briefly described. Before his successor, President Grant, had completed his first term, the incompetence of his administration, and a growing feeling that it was time for leniency towards the South, set off a revolt within his own party. Grant himself was neither dishonest nor vindictive, but he had no skill in politics, little interest in peacetime administration, and the old soldier's failing of loyalty to former comrades however unworthy. The result was inevitable. His period in office established a record of corruption which is still unequalled. A group of disillusioned Republicans broke away in 1872, and formed the Liberal Republican Party with the object of preventing Grant's re-election. They chose as their candidate Horace Greeley, a notable New York journalist and a man with a long record of interest in reform. Though Greeley had been a fierce critic of the Democratic Party, the Democrats, who in 1872 were still suffering from the taint of disloyalty which clung to them after the war, thought that their best chance of victory lay in joining with the Liberal Republicans. Greeley ran as a Democrat, and was heavily defeated. There were several reasons for his defeat. But, most important, his party was hopelessly heterogeneous. It contained free traders and protectionists, conservatives and radicals, reformers and machine politicians, united only by hostility to Grant and desire for office. Such a group had few positive reforms to advance. They wanted only a return to established decencies which had broken down under wartime strains and wartime opportunities. So limited a programme had limited appeal.

Left: *An attack on organised labour—union leaders Samuel Gompers and John Mitchell stir the cauldron of unionism*

Yet in one sense the Liberal Republicans were not completely defeated. So far as their movement had been a protest against governmental corruption, the country approved and the politicians read the signs. In 1876 both parties thought it well to choose presidential candidates known to be honest. The Republicans chose Rutherford Hayes, an effective Governor of Ohio, and the Democrats picked Samuel Tilden, Governor of New York, who had an even better record than Hayes as an active reformer who had successfully attacked political corruption in New York City. The election was hard fought; each party accused the other of malpractices. Hayes was ultimately declared the victor, for he had a majority of one in the electoral college, though Tilden had a clear majority of the popular vote. The manner of Hayes's victory, regarded as dubious even by many Republicans, damaged the cause of reform by lessening the new President's moral authority. Although he tried to restrict the so-called 'spoils system'—that is, to reduce the number of civil service positions in the gift of politicians and to increase the number of those filled by merit—he could not get far. The Civil Service Commission which took the first steps, feeble though they were, towards establishing a merit system, was not set up until 1883. (And even that piece of legislation required the assassination of a President, the unfortunate James Garfield, by a disappointed office-seeker.)

All this may seem to indicate a clear defeat for the forces of reform. In fact it was less than that. The 'spoils system' was hallowed in American politics. Politicians who had won an election thought it their right to find jobs and perquisites for their friends—and so did those friends. The system had something to recommend it. First, it could be argued that when an election had been won it made no sense to leave official posts in the hands of political enemies, whose loyalty and energy in carrying out policy would be at least open to question. Moreover, the system provided a necessary link, for which an alternative was hard to find, between political candidates whose ambitions were national, and their supporters whose interests were simply local. Still further, too much rectitude was priggish. It tended to set the politician above his constituents. It smacked of aristocracy, and was opposed for that reason. If knowing the right people helped a man to gain an office, where was the harm in that? Someone was bound to gain the office. Democracy required only that the chance of office should be widely available. Politicians ought to bribe their constituents—it is what they are for—but not too much. The reformers succeeded not by changing the system, but by improving agreed standards of political conduct. After 1872 it was accepted that presidential candidates must be men of integrity. When the Republicans nominated James G. Blaine in 1884, he lost the election in part because he was thought to fail that test. But the demand for honest government did something to keep government weak. Reformers believed that only government power made corruption possible. Corruption would be controlled more effectively by denying the government the power to help its friends than it would be by reliance on honest politicians. When, in the Progressive period, the demand for civil service reform was raised again, it was stimulated not by the desire for more honesty but by the desire for more competence.

Greenbacks and silver

Wartime policy had two other important consequences which extended into the peacetime years. First, the government had financed the war largely by borrowing, and had issued much paper currency. An inflated paper currency called for reform if the country were to return to the gold standard, as most men agreed that it should. But how was the reform to be accomplished without damage to one section of the community or unfair advantage to another? Though many Americans demanded a return to gold, others, especially Western farmers, wanted an even greater increase in the supply of money, and hence an increase in paper currency. The debate continued for years, recurring in various forms. During the post-war boom the problem was hardly an urgent one, but when depression struck in 1873, debt-ridden farmers formed the Greenback Party, to work for the issue of more paper money, conventionally known as 'greenbacks'. So far from making any concessions, conservatives struck back with the Resumption Act of 1875 which provided that the Treasury would redeem greenbacks in gold. The Greenback Party put up a presidential candidate in 1876, but its chief success was in the mid-term elections of 1878 when, as the Greenback-Labor Party, it polled more than one million votes and elected fourteen representatives. In that year Congress made the remaining greenbacks a permanent part of the currency. By the presidential election of 1880 the Greenback Party was already in decline, and it quietly faded away. When the currency question again came to the fore, it did so in a different form. Large deposits of silver had been dis-

Left: Presidents between the Civil and Spanish-American Wars: 1 Andrew Johnson (1865-69). 2 Ulysses Grant (1869-77). 3 Rutherford Hayes (1877-81). 4 J.A.Garfield (1881). 5 Chester Arthur (1881-85). 6 Grover Cleveland (1885-89, 1893-97). 7 Benjamin Harrison (1889-93). 8 William McKinley (1897-1901)

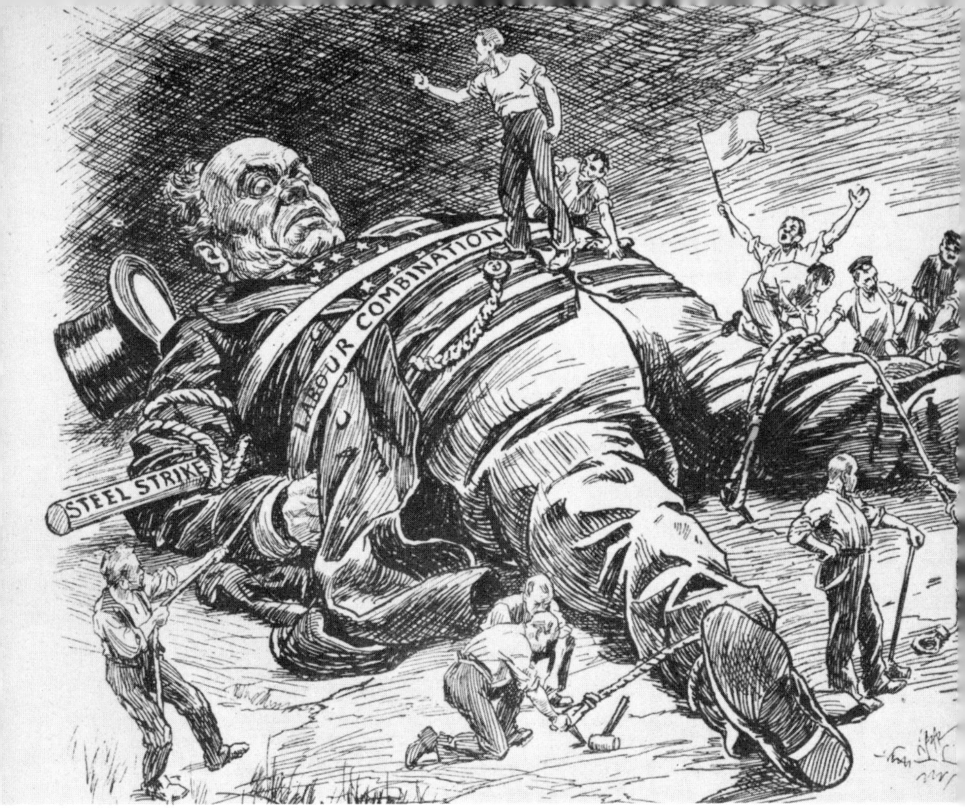
LABOUR COMBINATION
STEEL STRIKE

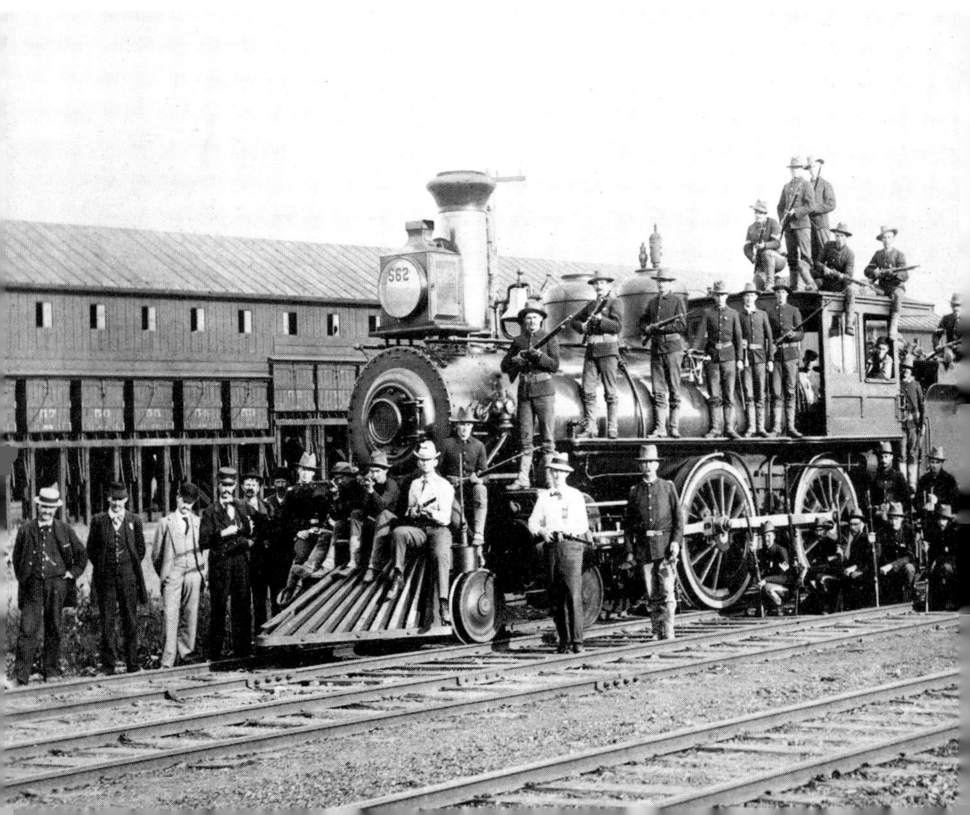
562

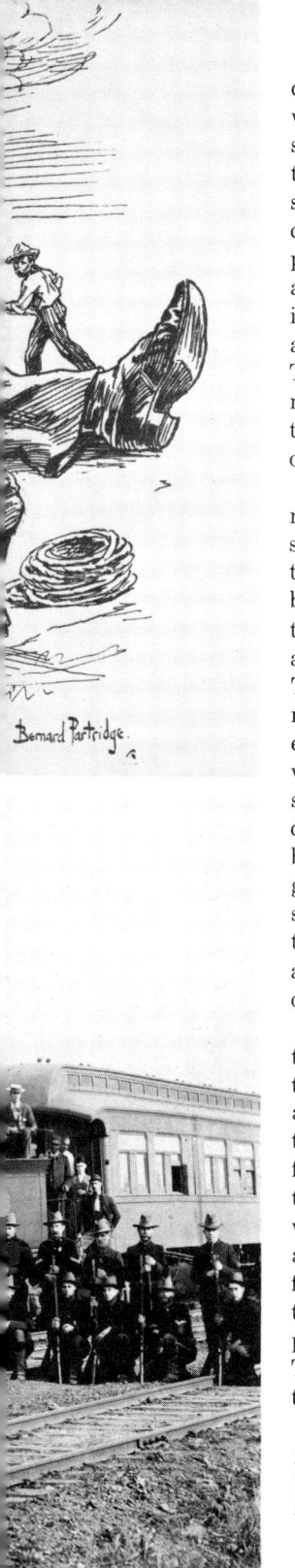

covered in the American West, and the debate was over whether the United States should base its currency on silver equally with gold, and on what the relationship between the value of the two metals ought to be. This version of the controversy—the demand for 'free silver'—came to a head at the same time as a wider movement of protest by Western farmers. At that point it ceased to be an argument merely about currency and took on larger implications. For the moment it is enough to note that an expanding economy paid for the cost of the Civil War. The burden of national debt, which had looked very formidable and dangerous in 1865, looked much less so twenty years later, though efforts to reduce it had been only partially successful.

An equally direct effect of the war was the establishment of a protective tariff. Before the war the Southern states, selling their cotton in a world market and anxious to buy manufactured goods as cheaply as possible, had been the strongest advocates of free trade; with the war, their influence was removed. At the same time there were arguments for protection which had not existed before. The country needed revenue, and American industries now suffering from a range of new wartime taxes were entitled to compensatory protection. At the end of the war it was generally assumed that a return to the old situation would follow, but it was natural to remove the domestic taxes first and see what effect that had before removing the tariff. The post-war prosperity was gratifying. The tariff produced a large surplus and it seemed folly to throw away such a national bonus. The tariff enabled the federal government to be carried on, and substantial pensions to be paid to war veterans, without requiring much in the way of federal domestic taxation.

In time the tariff came under question. It was argued that it gave the big industrial trusts a degree of protection which they did not need and which simply enabled them to make huge unearned profits. At the same time it was damaging American farmers by denying foreign customers the chance of earning sufficient dollars to buy their produce. The tariff became a party issue when the South, solidly attached to the Democratic Party, again began to campaign for lower tariffs. But tariff reform proved difficult. The desire of many Congressmen to protect some local interest led to that complicated political bargaining which Americans call 'log-rolling'. The duties which could muster support, which were also the duties that mattered, stayed high. The McKinley

Left, top: *A British cartoon of 1901 represents the American industrial giant held down by labour unrest.* **Bottom:** *Troops guard the railroads during the great Pullman strike of 1894*

tariff of 1890 was high, the Wilson-Gorman tariff of 1894, despite the best efforts of a Democratic President, Grover Cleveland, was higher, the Dingley tariff of 1897 higher still. By unhappy coincidence, the decade of the 1890s was the first since the Civil War in which the federal government's expenditure on average exceeded its receipts. The tariff could now be defended as a necessary means of raising revenue, and the more so because certain other means were not available. The Wilson-Gorman tariff act also contained a section levying a federal income tax of two per cent on incomes above four thousand dollars a year. That provision was quickly declared unconstitutional by the Supreme Court.

The political system

The process by which the discontents of America were made known and (sometimes) remedied was not a simple one. American politics has always been the politics of pressure groups, and the generalisation is hardly weakened when one adds that some, and some of the most effective, pressure groups are regional. (In a sense the solid South, always attached to the Democratic Party yet increasingly out of sympathy with the majority ideas of that party, was only the most specialised form of pressure group.) This regional basis of politics goes back to the origin of the country, in the thirteen states which were antecedent to the Union itself. The Senate is composed of men who are representatives of their states; the House of Representatives is composed almost entirely of men who represent parts of states. The President himself, though nationally elected, wins elections by accumulating majorities within a sufficient number of states. And, no less important, the federal government, though operating directly on the people, does so in rivalry or co-operation with state governments, independently elected, which also operate directly on the people.

These facts are in the nature of a federal system. They imply, among many other implications, that any man who wants to make his name in national politics must make it first in local and state politics. Very occasionally a war hero—a Grant or an Eisenhower—may gain the presidency without earlier political experience. Such exceptions do hardly more than prove the rule. The critical point in a politician's career comes when he must move out from his local, state base and become a national figure. It is critical because he has made his way so far by appealing to a restricted group of Americans, often by emphasising that which sets them apart from other Americans. Now he must somehow broaden his appeal to include most of the country. But he must do this without losing his own regional appeal, for if he loses that he

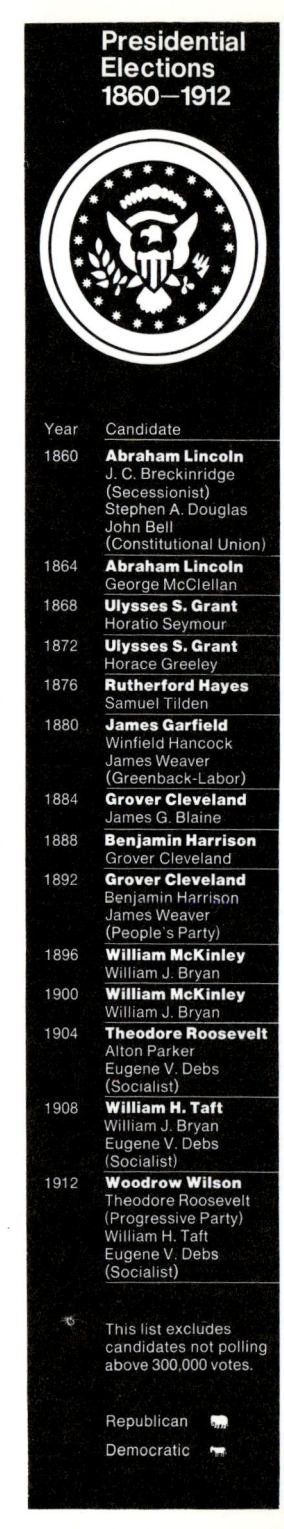

Presidential Elections 1860–1912

Year	Candidate
1860	**Abraham Lincoln** J. C. Breckinridge (Secessionist) Stephen A. Douglas John Bell (Constitutional Union)
1864	**Abraham Lincoln** George McClellan
1868	**Ulysses S. Grant** Horatio Seymour
1872	**Ulysses S. Grant** Horace Greeley
1876	**Rutherford Hayes** Samuel Tilden
1880	**James Garfield** Winfield Hancock James Weaver (Greenback-Labor)
1884	**Grover Cleveland** James G. Blaine
1888	**Benjamin Harrison** Grover Cleveland
1892	**Grover Cleveland** Benjamin Harrison James Weaver (People's Party)
1896	**William McKinley** William J. Bryan
1900	**William McKinley** William J. Bryan
1904	**Theodore Roosevelt** Alton Parker Eugene V. Debs (Socialist)
1908	**William H. Taft** William J. Bryan Eugene V. Debs (Socialist)
1912	**Woodrow Wilson** Theodore Roosevelt (Progressive Party) William H. Taft Eugene V. Debs (Socialist)

This list excludes candidates not polling above 300,000 votes.

Republican
Democratic

Party	Electoral College Votes	Popular Votes
🐘	180	1,865,593
🐘	72	848,356
🐘	12	1,382,713
🐘	39	592,906
🐘	212	2,206,938
🐘	21	1,803,787
🐘	214	3,013,421
🐘	80	2,706,829
🐘	286	3,596,745
🐘		2,843,446
🐘	185	4,036,572
🐘	184	4,284,020
🐘	214	4,453,295
🐘	155	4,414,082
		308,578
🐘	219	4,879,507
🐘	182	4,850,293
🐘	233	5,447,129
🐘	168	5,537,857
🐘	277	5,555,426
🐘	145	5,182,690
	22	1,029,846
🐘	271	7,102,246
🐘	176	6,492,559
🐘	292	7,218,491
🐘	155	6,356,734
🐘	336	7,628,461
🐘	140	5,084,223
		402,283
🐘	321	7,675,320
🐘	162	6,412,294
		420,793
🐘	435	6,296,547
	88	4,118,571
🐘	8	3,486,720
		900,672

cannot hope to gain anything more. Sometimes the task is simply impossible, as before the Civil War, when the sectional gap was too wide to be bridged. But even in happier times it is not easy. Presidents traditionally come from large states. From these, as nominees, they can bring to the campaign the largest number of 'safe' votes. But more than that, if they have made their way in large states they have proved themselves acceptable to a population not only larger but also more various than that of thinly-populated states. The larger the state the more likely it is to be, within limits, a microcosm of the nation.

Conversely, the smaller the state in population, the more likely it is to have needs, or a character, or both which set it somewhat apart from the country as a whole. The policy most acceptable to such a state is less likely to be that most acceptable to the country as a whole. The variety of the United States has always been part of the reason for the weakness of its national government. As the population of the nation has grown, regionalism has declined. During the late 19th and early 20th centuries it was probably at its height. A whole range of new states, thinly settled though large in area, were in process of being added to the Union until by 1912, when Arizona was admitted, the continental territory was finally completely divided into states. The effect was a range of states, and a number of thinly populated states, greater than the country had known hitherto. Although these thinly settled states, by reason of their low population, could not yet pull their full political weight, they had a large potential for obstruction, especially in the Senate where they had equal representation with any other. Nor were the differences only between old states and new states, populous states and thinly-populated states. The new states differed no less than the old in their wealth and natural resources.

Yet if the variety of the country inhibited action by the national government, it might be supposed to have left the way clear for action by state governments. Indeed protest movements were, as they still are for the most part, local in origin. The first task of any reformer is to develop and demonstrate the local support—the 'grassroots support'— which will attract the interest of more influential politicians. The growth of political movements among Western farmers demonstrates the point. The Granger movement, named after the National Grange of the Patrons of Husbandry, which had 59 ▷

Left: Republican America—the 'Grand Old Party' held power for all but eight years between 1860-1912. **Next page:** An Industrial Workers of the World meeting. The I.W.W. challenged both American capitalism and conventional reformist unions

IRISH
SOCIALIST CLUB
Fas a Bealac
CLEAR THE WAY
ALL GOOD AND TRUE IRISHMEN
UP MEN A
INDUSTRIAL
ORGANIZATION
NEW YORK
DISTRICT
HEADQUARTERS

UNITY CLU
SEMPRE AVANTI
SOCIALISM IN OUR TI

RKERS OF THE WORLD.
ON, EMANCIPATION,
INDUSTRIAL
COUNCIL
COOPER SQUARE

THE "PAST" HAS HONORE
ITS MILITARY HEROES"
THE FUTURE
WILL HONOR ITS INDUSTRIAL
HEROES
THERE ARE THOUSANDS
WALKING THE STREETS AT NIGHT
WITHOUT SHELTER
WHAT IS THE MUNICIPAL
LODGING HOUSE FOR?
THE RIGHT TO WORK!
SHALL BE GUARANTEED
TO ALL CITIZENS
REGARDLESS OF
CREED, COLOR
OR SEX.
ITS COMING YET.
FOR A' THAT.
THAT, MAN TO MAN THE WORLD O'ER
SHALL BROTHERS BE
AND A' THAT.

WE DEMAND
8 HOURS
WORK DAY!
SEC
1
IN UNITY
IS OUR STRENGTH
LUNIONE
fo LA FORZA
LAVORATORI
O IL MONDO
ITEVI.
WE WANT
8 HOURS
WORK
PANTS MAKERS
UNION

been formed in 1867 as a social and educational association of farmers in the Middle West, grew naturally into an organised protest against economic abuses. As early as 1871 the state of Illinois set up a commission to fix maximum charges for the storage and transport of grain. Wisconsin and Iowa followed with railway legislation in 1874; by that time farmers' parties had been formed in eleven states. The difficulty for farmers' leaders was always that of sustaining interest when times improved. The Granger movement faded when the Greenback movement, already mentioned, distracted attention. But in the later 1880s the farm regions of the Middle West suffered a much more serious depression, originating in drought, and farm revolt flared again. The Farmers' Alliances now took over from the Grange as centres of organisation. They too worked first and by choice on the state rather than on the national level, for the practical reason that state action was easier, was a necessary preliminary to national action, and might be effective enough to make national action unnecessary. They organised farmers' exchanges and co-operative marketing schemes, and through their newspapers and magazines they identified the common grievances of farmers and built up support for common remedies.

Farmers' movements took the form they did because there was always a substantial number of states which were predominantly rural and agricultural. The industrial workers had no such natural bases. There were early attempts at political action: the Socialist Labor Party was formed in 1877, as an attempt to develop a national party from a workingmen's party which had achieved some success in New York City. It was always riven by dissension, especially after Daniel De Leon, a prickly and intransigent Marxist, took over the leadership in the 1890s. The moderates broke away from the party in 1899 to form the Social Democratic Party, later the Socialist Party. This had some success: its presidential candidate, Eugene Debs, polled over 900,000 votes in 1912, some 6 per cent of the total. Such a vote, of course, gave the party no chance of national success. It may be more significant that in local elections at about the same time the Socialists carried eighteen cities and almost won several more. The main efforts of the workers, however, were through trade unions. In the United States these went back to a shoemakers' union in Philadelphia in 1792. After the Civil War, national organisations of unions were formed. In the early years the dominant body

Left, top: *Parade of unemployed, 1909. The unions embraced many ethnic groups.* **Bottom:** *Garment workers on strike—the signs are written in English, Italian, Hebrew, and Russian*

was the Knights of Labor, tightly organised by industries under the leadership of Terence Powderly, and with membership open to all workers. Powderly had some victories. In 1884 the Knights organised a railway strike which forced even Jay Gould to come to terms. Eventually, however, it became clear that the national organisation was too rigid for effective action. A famous Chicago riot — the Haymarket Riot of 1886 — did much to damage the Knights of Labor, and in that year the American Federation of Labor was formed which, giving much more autonomy to individual unions, quickly took over the leadership of the American labour movement. There was a price to pay. The founder and first president of the AF of L, Samuel Gompers, was quite willing to use strikes and boycotts as a means of enforcing collective bargaining, but he was opposed to political action and, it was charged, he gained benefits for skilled workers only by abandoning any concern for the unskilled. The American labour movement was split until long after the First World War between the conservative wing led by Gompers and the radicals who wanted political action. If the test is that of immediate results, there can be little doubt that Gompers was right. Most employers were strongly hostile to unions, and such gains as the workers made were by strike action now in one industry, now in another. Action on a national scale, even within a single industry, rarely succeeded. The powerful American Railway Union, for example, with some successes against railway companies already behind it, failed dramatically in its strike in 1894, against the company which made Pullman railway carriages, because its tactics involved a boycott of the carriages throughout the country and so was held to threaten both the working of the railways and the transport of the mail.

Muckrakers and social workers

Farmers and workers were organising to advance their own interests. Increasingly, however, reformers were becoming concerned with the fate of those less fortunate than themselves. As the cities grew, there were people who noticed the evils that grew with them. It took time for these reformers to make their mark. The term 'muckraker' was coined in 1906 to apply to the journalists who sought out abuses and wrote highly-coloured accounts of them in popular magazines. They were indeed one of the mainsprings of the Progressive movement. But they had their forerunners much earlier, and the abuses they described were real certainly enough. They attacked the practices of big business — H.D.Lloyd exposed the methods of Standard Oil as early as 1881 — but increasingly they also tackled the problems of urban life. This was a field

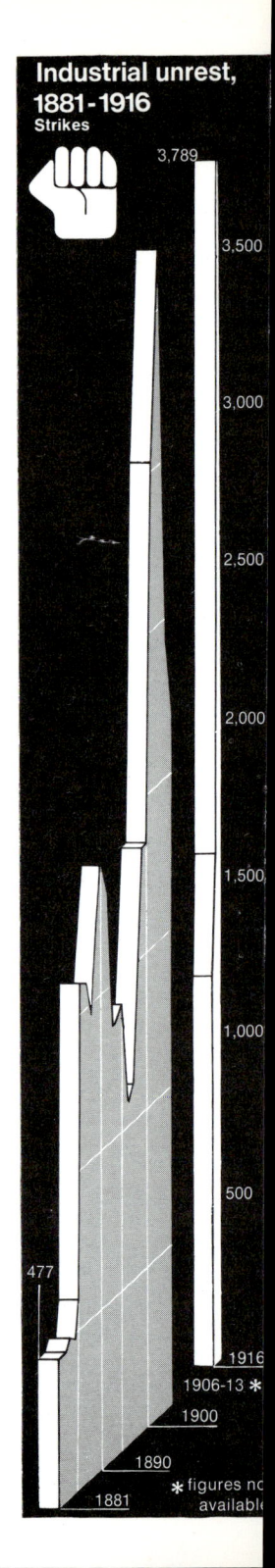

Industrial unrest, 1881-1916
Strikes

3,789
3,500
3,000
2,500
2,000
1,500
1,000
500
477
1916
1906-13 *
1900
1890
1881

* figures no available

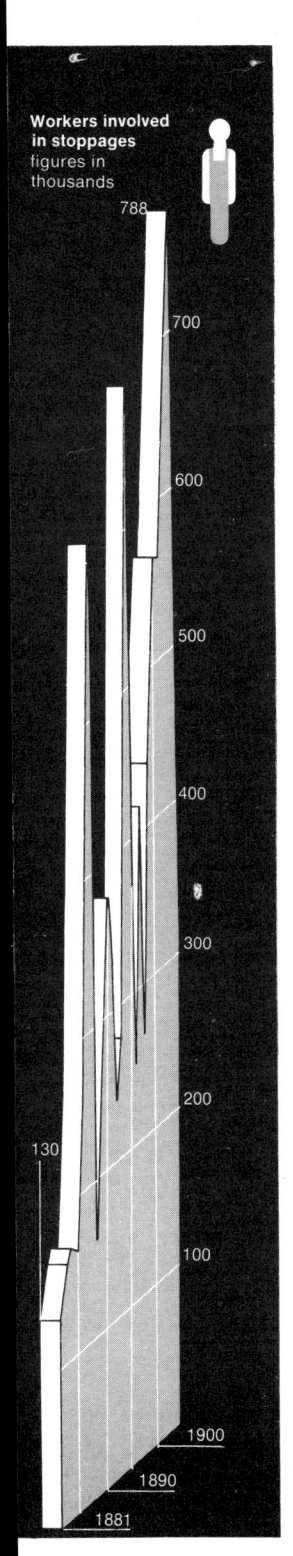

Workers involved in stoppages
figures in thousands

788
700
600
500
400
300
200
130
100
1900
1890
1881

in which women were especially active, and it was also one in which American reformers learned much from Europe. One important development was that of the social settlements in the slums of the cities. Perhaps the best known of these was Hull House in Chicago, founded by Jane Addams in 1889 on the model of Toynbee Hall in London. But there were many others. What made the social settlements important was less their charitable work than the part they played in bringing together and educating the very remarkable group of people who worked in them. They tackled a whole range of problems — slum housing, adulterated food, prostitution, the exploitation of child labour — and in their efforts they learned, slowly and sometimes painfully, what sorts of action were effective and what were not.

The demands of protesting groups in the 1870s and 1880s did not go altogether unheeded. The Interstate Commerce Act, for example, was passed in 1887 as an attempt to regulate the activities of railways. Weak instrument though it was, it provided a basis from which further developments could later be made. The demands of farmers and others for easier credit and a less restricted money supply also gained some concessions. Nevertheless, in the late 'eighties and early 'nineties the protests grew louder and louder. Between 1892 and 1896 the Democratic President Cleveland was in office. Notoriously conservative, he did as little as any man could to mitigate the depression of those years. The presidential election of 1896 became a real struggle between radicals and conservatives, and it was savagely fought. The victor was William McKinley, a Republican, whose first purpose was to heal the sectional bitterness revealed by the election and to reunite the country. Fortunately for him and for the country, prosperity returned. McKinley was re-elected in 1900. But in 1901 an anarchist's bullet cut him down and brought to the presidency Theodore Roosevelt, a man whose vision of the office was altogether more dynamic.

Left: *Even in the home of rugged individualism the industrial worker was learning to find security — and profit — in numbers*

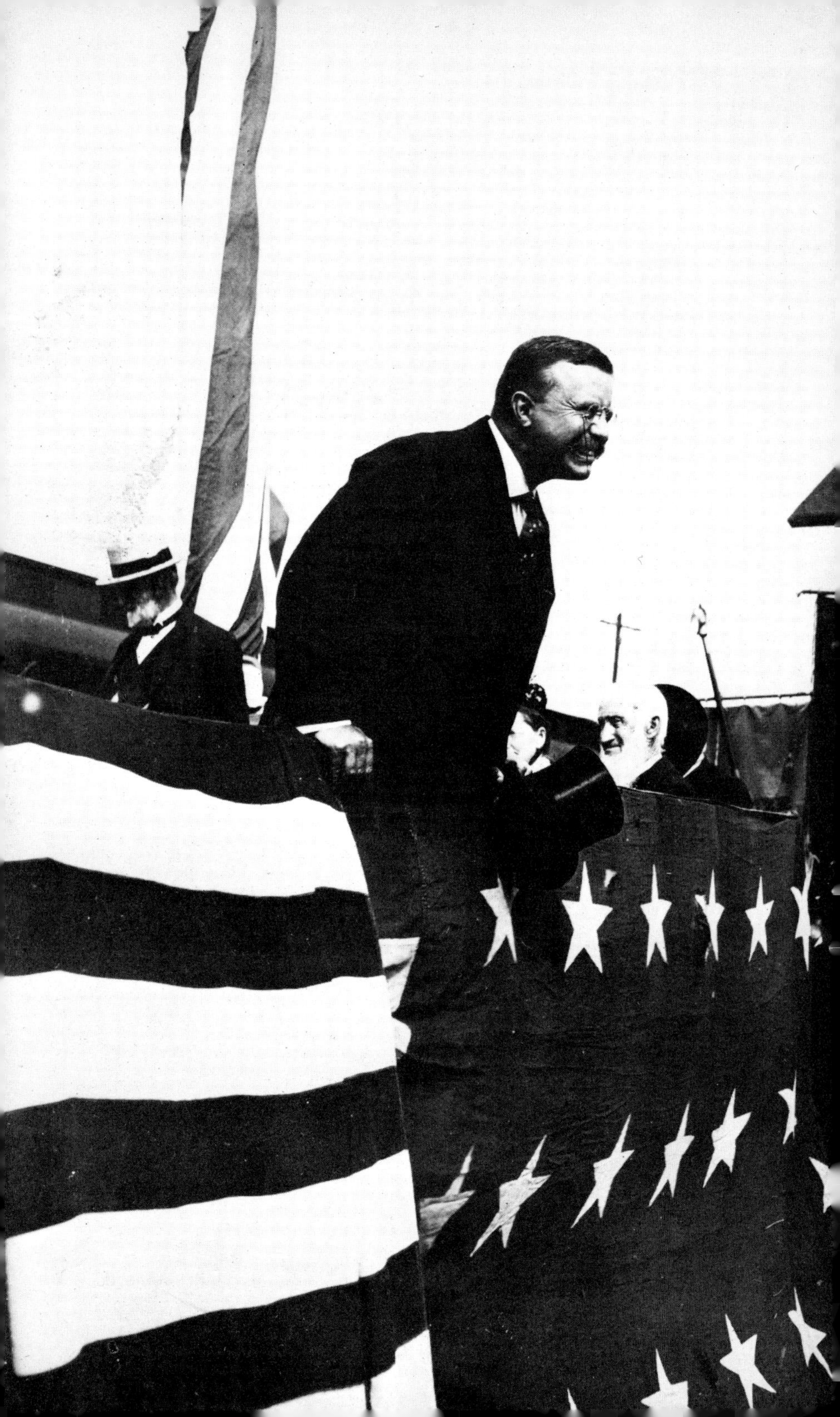

Chapter 4
Theodore Roosevelt and the Progressive Movement

Theodore Roosevelt is one of those political figures whose importance rests above all on their personality, and on their position in the political setting of their time. To these we must now turn. He was born in New York in 1858. The strongest influence on his early life was his father. The older Roosevelt was not himself a political figure of note but he was a remarkable man. He made a substantial fortune in business and then decided to retire. He was a devout churchman, keenly concerned for a whole range of good causes in and around New York. Upright, pious, worthy, philanthropic, nothing is known to his discredit and much to his credit. He was, in short, just the sort of person whom moderns tend to approach with distrust and with more than a little dislike. They would be wrong. Roosevelt's father was also kindly, warmhearted, and fun. His son liked him, enjoyed his company, and acquired from him a zest for life which never deserted him. But the young Roosevelt was a weakly child, suffering from asthma and never strong. In reaction to this, he set about building himself up physically. There was a limit to what a man of Roosevelt's physique could accomplish, but what he could he did. He became a fitness fiend, forever testing himself in boxing and other sports. He became a fanatic for the outdoors, a devotee of the wilderness and the West, a rider, an explorer, a big game hunter. In the presidency his fondness for capturing diplomats or cabinet officers and sweeping them off on gruelling hikes across rough country became notorious. And so did his high regard for those who could keep up with him or who took their discomfiture in good part.

Roosevelt's education was otherwise conventional enough – a private boarding school, Harvard, some study of law – the standard background of an American gentleman. But then his career took a very unusual course: he went into politics. At that time, in 1881, politics was not a career for a gentleman. It was too crude and too corrupt. Gentlemen stood on the sidelines and deplored the political jungle. Or they intervened, if they did so at all,

Left: *President 'TR' on the stump, Brattleboro, Vermont, 1903*

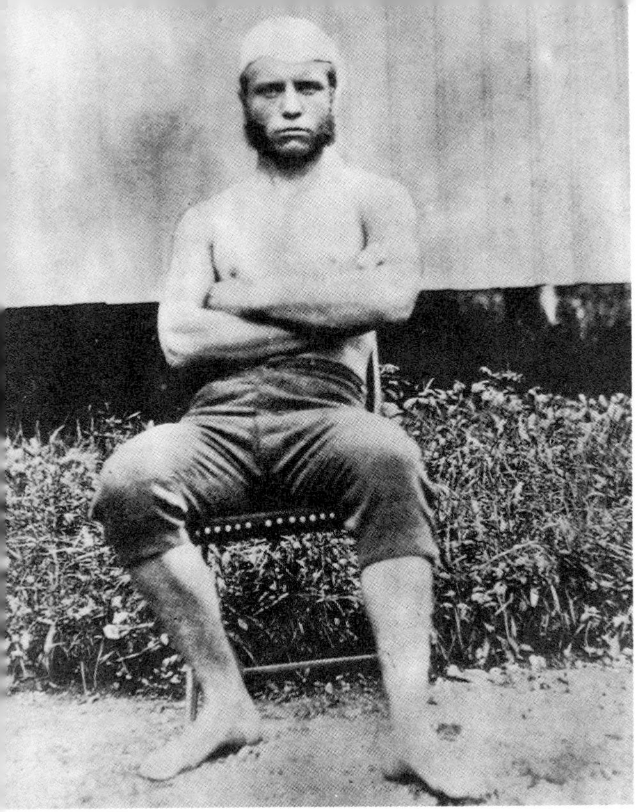

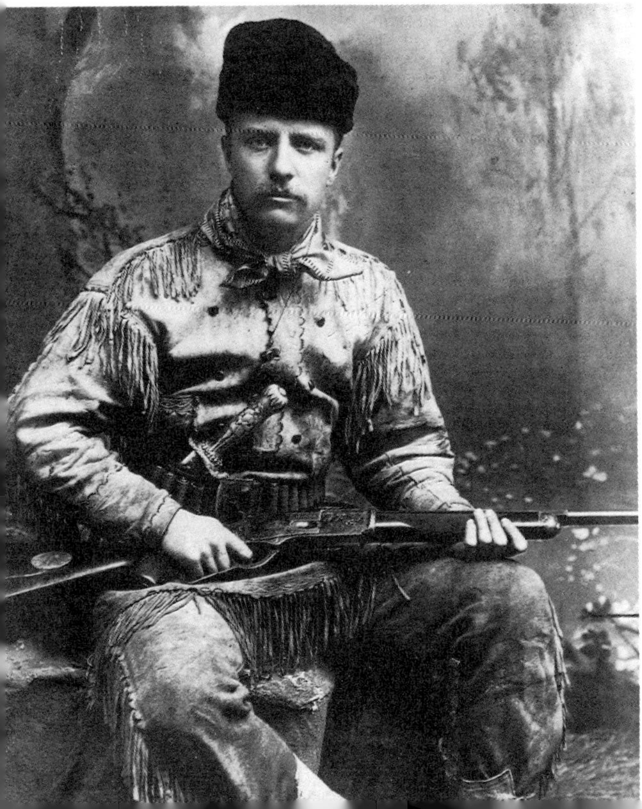

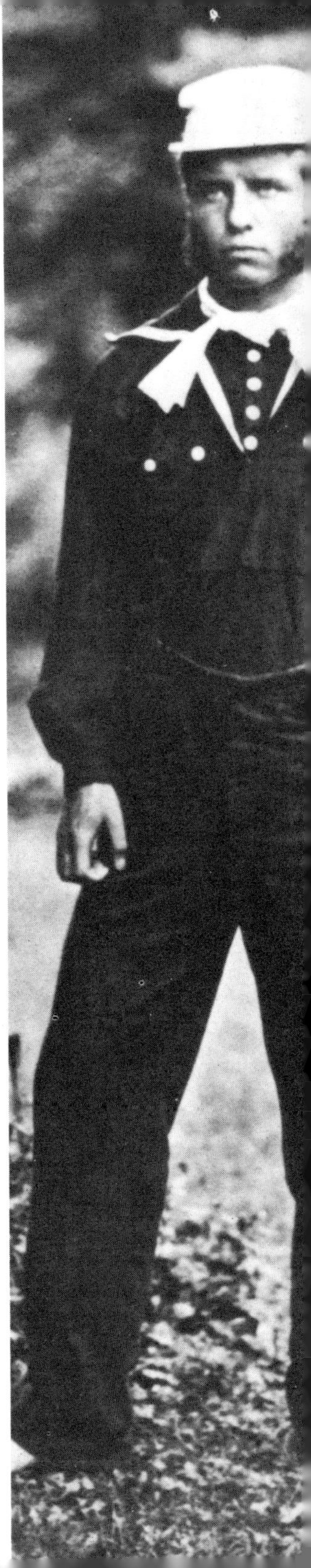

by occasional bursts of organised outrage designed to force the politicians to behave with rather more discretion. Roosevelt ran for the New York State Assembly with misgivings, and with the idea that he would not stay if he did not like it. His first experiences were depressing. He found politics just what his friends had always told him it was. But he stayed; he was hooked. He stayed because he liked power, and because he came to see that only through effective political action could reform be brought about; which of these motives was more important, no one can say. The desire to reform and the determination to be effective — the sense that only in reform can one's effectiveness be measured — ran together through TR's entire career. One other political lesson Roosevelt learned early, that of party loyalty. In 1884 the Republican candidate for President was James G. Blaine, a man whose political talents were matched by his reputation for corruption. Many Republican gentlemen could not stomach Blaine and deserted the party, ensuring the first Democratic presidential victory since the Civil War, and giving the term 'Mugwump' to the language as a permanent name for one whose stomach is too queasy for politics. Roosevelt hesitated, but finally swallowed his distaste, and stayed with the party. His later career would have been different had he done otherwise.

The reformer
Political defeat and the death of his first wife in 1884 sent Roosevelt for two years to the West where he owned a ranch in what was then the Dakota Territory. His knowledge of, and love for, the West and its history — of which he wrote an account in six volumes — and his ability to deal with the sort of men who settled the region were important in Roosevelt's later career. But his political base remained, as it had to remain, in the East. His first national experience was as a member of the Civil Service Commission. In the United States, as in other countries, the creation of a professional civil service was a slow and painful business, opposed by politicians to whom patronage was a source of power. Even when the Civil Service Commission was established, its initial scope was not very wide. Roosevelt himself as President was later to take the lead in extending it. But, in its early days, membership of the Commission was the sort of job which called not merely for honesty and energy, but perhaps above all for tact.

As we have seen, the growing hostility to corruption

Left: The making of a President. Far left, top: The college athlete. Left: The student. Far left, bottom: Dressed to kill

was probably the most immediate stimulus to reform after the Civil War. When Roosevelt left the Civil Service Commission in 1895 he became Police Commissioner of New York City. The police force of a major city and major port, dominated by an entrenched political machine, was a fertile field for corruption, and an honest, courageous Police Commissioner might well find he had his hands full. But corruption was not the only issue. Experience of police work in a crowded city brought home to Roosevelt, as work on the Civil Service Commission could not do, that important social problems had roots which honest administration could not reach. Some people had corruption forced on them. Legislative reform was needed. At the same time, this intimate experience of the lives of New York's poor strengthened Roosevelt's innate contempt for impractical men and impractical reformers. He became aware that many schemes for legislative improvement would fail simply because the men who drew them up lacked sufficient insight and sufficient knowledge of how the people for whom they were planning really lived. He also gained the strong sense that the search for perfection might be self-defeating. Better to win something than to lose all by asking too much.

Another source of Roosevelt's strength is revealed in his next move in 1897 back into national administration as Assistant Secretary of the Navy. Roosevelt never had to claw his way to national prominence through a long apprenticeship in local politics. From the start, the range of his connections was good enough to ensure that he might be called to office in Washington through his friendship with older and influential men in the Republican Party. The navy was a focus of interest and concern to Americans in the 1890s, as part of the growing concern with foreign policy with which we shall deal later. Roosevelt had early taken an interest in the navy, and had written on the subject. As Assistant Secretary he had scope for his enthusiasm. When the Spanish-American War broke out in 1898, the navy was in good shape, and its performance contrasted favourably with that of the army, which had suffered from years of neglect and complacency. For the state of the navy Roosevelt must certainly share some credit, especially since his superior, the Secretary of the Navy, John D. Long, was a gentle and not very effective figure.

Yet when the Spanish-American War broke out, Roosevelt resigned from the Navy Department. It is evidence of the informal and half-organised way in which military matters were then run that he did so in order to form and lead to Cuba a cavalry unit which he recruited in the West and which became known as the 'Rough Riders'. The unit performed well, with an informality, ingenuity, and dash which contrasted well with that of some regular formations and which captured the public imagination. It was in this episode that Roosevelt first showed the talent for publicity which was so marked later and which so enraged his opponents. He was certainly not modest about his role. Finlay Peter Dunne, a humorist whose Irish spokesman Mr Dooley commented trenchantly on the foibles of the whole era, suggested that Roosevelt's account of the war should be called *'Alone in Cubia'*. Roosevelt returned from the war a hero, and as a hero took the next step in his political career.

Kicked upstairs!
A man of Roosevelt's experience, character, and vigour was clearly to be reckoned with in the politics of New York State. The dominant figure in New York's Republican Party—the boss of the state Republican machine—was Senator T.C.Platt. He was shrewd enough to see that he might do better by working with Roosevelt than by waiting for a challenge from him, and took the lead in securing Roosevelt's nomination and election as Governor of the state. But he underestimated his man. Roosevelt had undertaken not to challenge Platt's control of the patronage of the state, and he kept his word. But he began a campaign for honest government which threatened to become embarrassing to the party machine. In his view Platt had acted out of self-interest and he, Roosevelt, owed him nothing. For Roosevelt, as for many men of his stamp, loyalty was a one-way street. No one was quicker to resent disloyalty, or to interpret a difference of opinion as disloyalty. After the very earliest stages of his career, Roosevelt could always persuade himself that where he was there was the party. In the struggle with Platt, Roosevelt had morality on his side. It began to look as if he might also have the public. Platt took refuge in an ancient resort—the attempt to kick Roosevelt upstairs. As the presidential election of 1900 approached, William McKinley, a Republican, was in office and conventionally entitled to renomination. Roosevelt, however, was ambitious enough to think that he had a chance to replace McKinley, and his ambition gave Platt the opportunity to work successfully for a very different result: that Roosevelt should be nominated for the vice-presidency. He was so nominated, the Republicans won again, and Roosevelt was elected—to a post which had increasingly become both a sinecure and a political dead end. Platt was rid of him. But then fate took a hand. In September 1901, McKinley was assassinated. Theodore Roosevelt became President. His accession may be taken

Left, top: *'That damned cowboy'*. **Bottom:** *On safari in Africa*

67

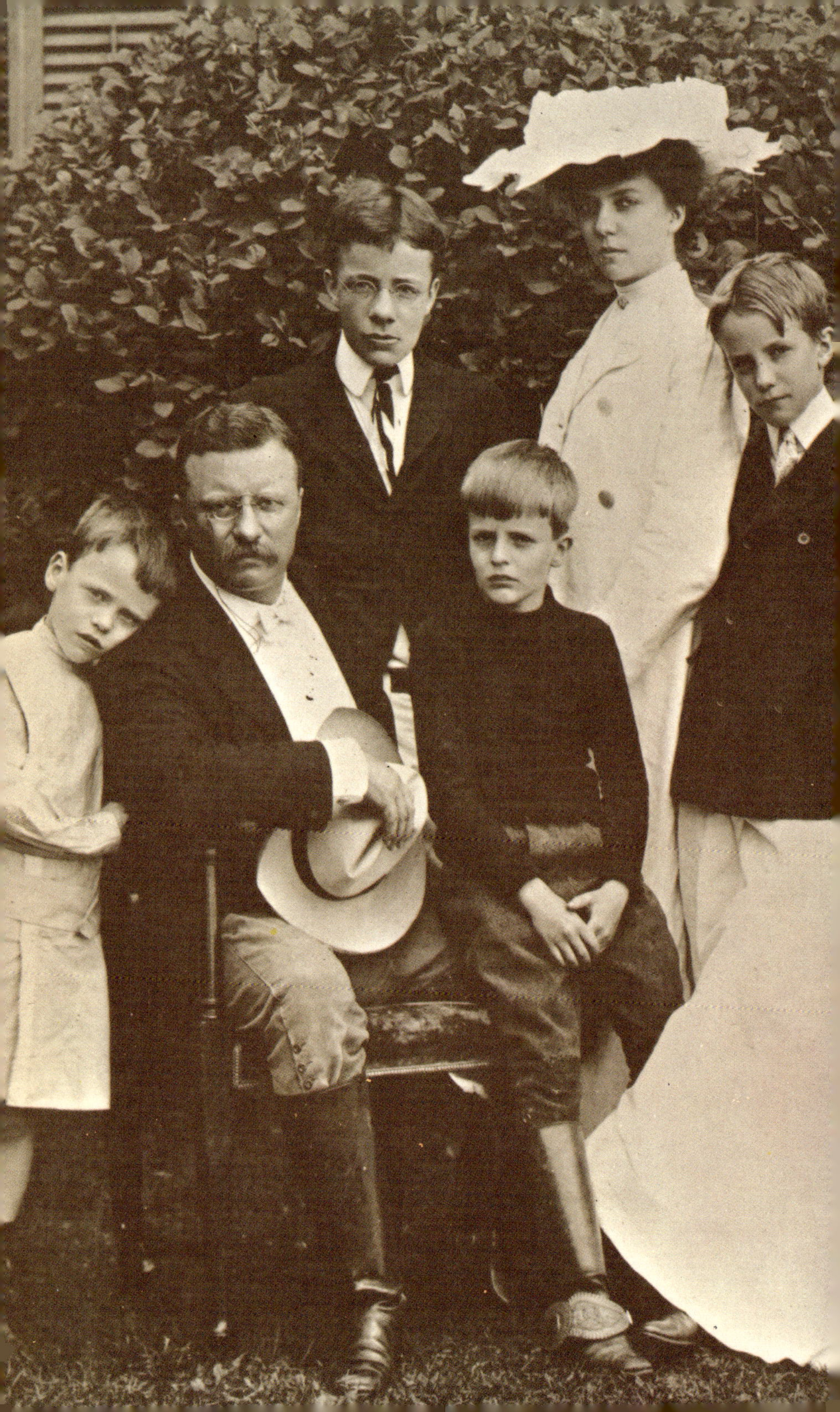

to inaugurate the beginning of the Progressive era.

Few questions in American history have given the historian more difficulty than the character of the Progressive movement. Its rise, its decline, and its essential nature, all raise problems. But something can be done to put it in its setting. The agrarian discontent which had been growing since the depression of the later 'eighties came to a national head between 1892 and 1896 in the so-called Populist Revolt. At the same time another movement had come to a head, the demand for 'free silver'. This rested on the belief that the economic ills of the country originated in a currency which was artificially restricted by keeping the country on the gold standard. The 'free silver' men argued that this policy must be the work of a small group of wealthy men acting in their own interest, because the remedy was available and obvious: expand the currency by basing it on silver, of which there was an ample supply in the United States, as well as on gold. The Democratic President of the depression years, Grover Cleveland, was as firmly committed to the gold standard as any Republican. In the mid-term elections of 1894 the Populists, building a temporary alliance of farmers and some industrial workers, had done well, though their centre of strength remained in the farming West. As the presidential election of 1896 approached, they hoped to draw dissidents from both the Republican and the Democratic parties, and make a real challenge under their leader William Jennings Bryan, a popular orator of enormous fervour and appeal but, so his opponents said, a demagogue and nothing more. What happened was rather different. The Democrats rejected their own President, who was so unpopular as to be a liability. Most of them went over to the doctrine of 'free silver', while the smaller 'sound money' rump temporarily allied with the Republicans. Bryan collected the seceders, and fought the election as a Democrat, at the head of a coalition of Democrats and Populists, on a platform which emphasised 'free silver' even at the cost of other reforms. Against this demagogue, preaching a policy which they considered would mean economic ruin, conservatives threw themselves into battle with a fury close to despair. Their campaign, though headed by McKinley, was run by a political organiser of genius, Mark Hanna, who had no hesitation in raising large sums from businessmen to fight off the challenge to their interests.

McKinley won, the 'free silver' forces had been routed for four years at least, and the country turned to other matters, such as the worsening situation in Cuba. McKinley was also helped by economic recovery, and by the

Left: *The family man—TR with his wife and children in 1903*

extreme fluidity of Western politics, which made it hard to sustain a challenge for long. In that struggle of 1896 many Eastern liberals had been for McKinley. McKinley himself was no mindless conservative, and neither was Hanna, a notably well-liked and enlightened mine-owner, with a keen sense of social responsibility as well as of self-interest. 'Any employer who won't meet his men half way,' he once said, 'is a plain damn fool.' They won liberal support, however, because of Bryan's defects rather than because of McKinley's merits. Many men who recognised that reform was needed thought that Bryan's panaceas were not the answer. In destroying privilege, they would destroy the whole economy. Moreover, whatever he intended, Bryan's campaign was bound to have the effect of setting class against class and region against region. He was too completely and exclusively the spokesman of the West, of the farmer, of the workingman, to make a President. That was hardly by intention. Bryan did what he could to wage a national campaign, and was a less dangerous figure than he seemed at the time. But by the nature of his career and his cause he could not build a wide enough following.

The appeal to nationalism
McKinley's talents were those of a peace maker. He was not a dynamic national leader. Rather he believed in what has recently been christened 'benign neglect'. The Populist challenge had had the effect of forcing many moderate reformers over to the side of conservatism. After McKinley's victory they again began to ask questions and make proposals. Four years later, with Roosevelt's succession, they found a leader. This short summary of events preceding Roosevelt's presidency does not make the definition of the Progressive movement much easier. But it points to some useful generalisations about its nature, wide though these must be. First, there was a strong nationalist strain in the movement. From early times, Americans had believed that their country possessed sound institutions, and even the Civil War had done little to shake that confidence. Bryan's campaign had appealed strongly to American nationalism and self-sufficiency — he had depicted the gold standard as an international bankers' ramp — and the men who had fought him because they thought his prescriptions dangerous were no less nationalistic than he. Indeed, one of their charges was that Bryan's campaign threatened to split the nation, and give it over to class and sectional conflict. Moreover, whatever the origins of Bryan's policies and emotions, many saw behind him the spectre of socialism, which was beginning to spread in Europe and from Europe into the United States. Though some Progressives were more

radical than others, and though there were some effective American socialist leaders, the main body of Progressive reformers were clear that reform must be in ways consonant with the American tradition, and must avoid the excesses of socialism. To give in to socialism, apart from anything else, would be to deny the validity of the political thought on which the Union had been founded. Men with a political religion of their own resisted conversion to another.

One object of reform, then, was to stave off socialism. In that sense the Progressive movement was both conservative and nationalistic. But Progressivism was nationalistic in another and perhaps a simpler sense. Agitators like Bryan, so it was feared, would weaken the country by splitting it. In an increasingly dangerous world, the United States could not afford that. The German Empire loomed as a new and altogether more formidable sort of state than had yet been seen; and behind Germany loomed such potentially yet more formidable competitors as Russia and China. Today we know that Americans much exaggerated the speed with which such states could modernise themselves and become effective international powers. That was not apparent then. In a dangerous world, reform must not weaken the United States. In fact, one chief object of Progressive reform was to increase the national strength. The government must be active and efficient. The people must be healthy and well educated. The economy must be strong; nothing must be done to inhibit its continued growth. Other powers must not be allowed to seize parts of the world which they could use against the United States. The armed forces must be strong and efficient enough to prevent that, and the government sufficiently alert to identify danger in time.

Popular backing

It would be wrong, however, to place the chief emphasis either on the nationalist or on the conservative aspect of Progressivism. The liberals who had rallied to the side of McKinley against a wild man from the West like Bryan were reformers none the less, and they reverted to the idea of reform as soon as it was safe to do so. They saw discontent and they recognised its justice. Different reformers gave priority to different reforms, and their variety has been a chief source of difficulty for historians. But that difficulty serves to emphasise another quality of the Progressive movement. It was genuinely popular in origin. It was not invented by an individual or even by a few men, and then presented to the public for approval. Rather a whole range of demands began to come together,

Left: *TR and the naturalist John Muir in Yosemite Valley*

from many different sources and contributed by men of widely differing characters and experience, until they formed a movement. It is by some such process that a period of reform, in any country, is always given its character. Politicians, in an open and complex society, were responding to demands rather than forming them. Their function was what it had always been, to hold together a coalition of support large enough to win a national election. Increasingly, only a reformer could hope to do that. Though intellectuals worked hard to provide the movement with a philosophy and to define its essence, their efforts were of secondary importance.

'Overmighty subjects'

However various the springs of reform were, a focus was early given to the movement not by agreement on its purposes but rather by the activities of those who resisted it. When men looked around and considered what was wrong with America, they might reach very different answers and even spend much of their time opposing each other; but they quickly agreed that some Americans had too much power—which, in America, meant essentially that they had too much wealth. These men were magnates not of land but of industry. We have seen how they built up the gigantic trusts in such basic American industries as railways, steel, and oil. Here was the starting point: how should one deal with the huge accumulations of wealth which industrial America was piling up in a few hands, and how with the rich men who devoted their energy, their ingenuity, and their riches to making themselves richer still? The complaint in a sense was still against corruption, but of a more sophisticated kind. Some men carried enough weight to see that their interests were protected, and in so doing they damaged the interests of millions of other Americans. The emphasis shifted away from the man who took the bribe to the man who offered it, offered it often in an entirely legal way, and who, in a sense, could hardly help offering it. The problem was that of what Tudor England would have called the 'overmighty subject'. But even if there was agreement about the problem, there was no agreement about the solution. To some modern historians the Progressives seem needlessly timid in their efforts, and to others even conservatives in disguise. It was a real difficulty that the idea of competition as the basis of commercial life and, in a sense, of social life also, with rewards for the successfully competitive, was one of the foundations of American political philosophy. The most important charge against the trusts was that they were so powerful that they prevented competition. They could crush any new rival before he had the strength to face them. That was unfair. That was what made them 'overmighty'. Yet the trusts were clearly themselves in some sense the products of competition, the ultimate victors in the business struggle. To attack them would be to rob men of their prize simply for being successful. That too would be unfair. And it might be dangerous. Americans have learned in a long political history that to be unscrupulous in a good cause invites others to be unscrupulous in a bad one.

Legal recourse
The belief in competition was given an edge in the later 19th century by the doctrine usually called Social Darwinism, the belief that in society, as in nature, conflict is beneficial because it results in the survival of the fittest and the elimination of weaklings. Reformers who wanted to tackle the trusts had to tackle that doctrine. As they tried to do so, they found it upheld in law. It quickly became clear to them that, in certain respects at least, they had to work on a national level. In a federal system, under which two potentially rival governments—national and state—may affect the same population, it is necessary to have some instrument for adjudicating between them. In the United States that instrument is the Constitution, ultimately interpreted by the Supreme Court. Much therefore depended on the attitude of the Justices of the Supreme Court. For some years after the Civil War the Court seemed set on a liberal course, upholding the Granger laws, for example, on the ground of their social utility. But in the middle 'eighties the Court began to reverse earlier decisions, and for the rest of the century took a notably conservative line against any interference by legislation with business practice.

Two main weapons were available to conservatives. The Constitution had given Congress the right to regulate commerce among the states, and had specifically prohibited the states from certain actions which might damage the wellbeing of other states. As the railway network spread across the country, and as commerce followed where the railway network led, it became possible for ingenious lawyers to argue that almost any state law touching industry or commerce infringed the clause of the Constitution laying down that interstate commerce was a matter for the federal government alone. Wide though the power given to the Court by the interstate **76** ▷

Left: The rising politician. **Top:** *Roosevelt rides the bucking bronco of the spoils system as a Civil Service Commissioner, 1889-95.* **Bottom:** *TR, Assistant Secretary of the Navy, 1897-98.* **Next page:** *Progressive anti-trust cartoon of 1902—Congressional action illuminates the misdeeds of the capitalists*

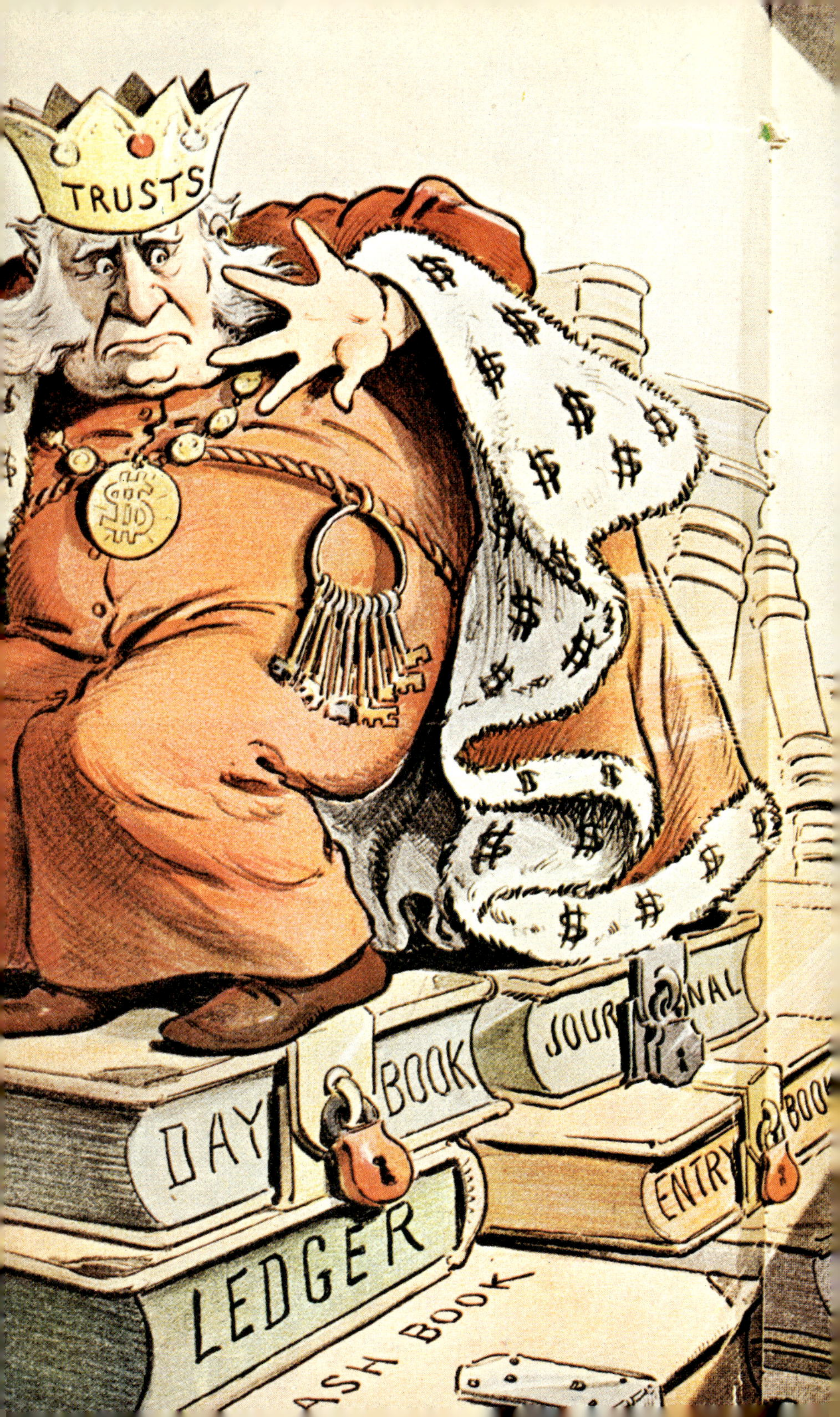
TRUSTS
DAY
BOOK
JOUR
NAL
ENTRY
LEDGER
ASH BOOK

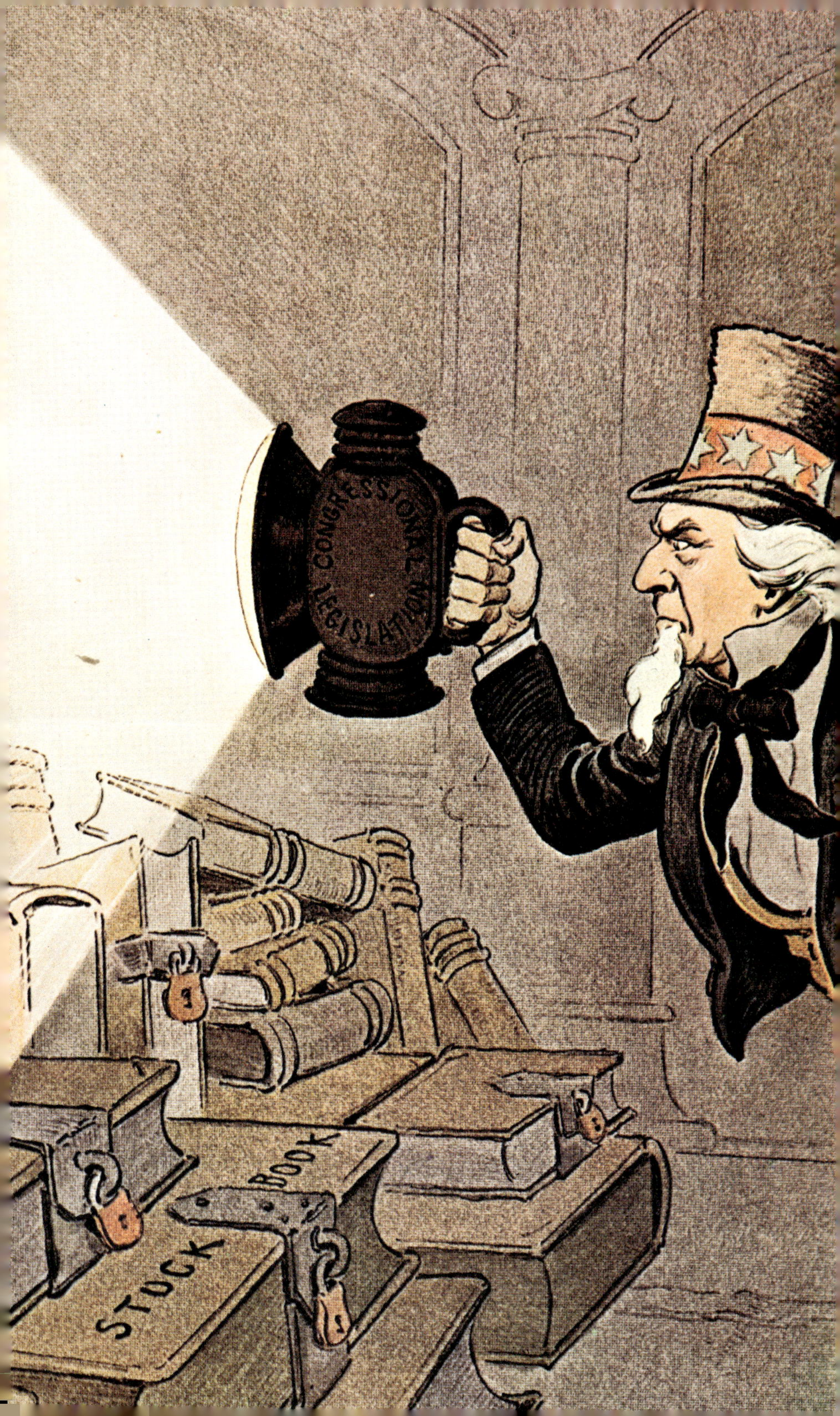
CONGRESSIONAL INV. LEGISLATION
BOOK
STOCK

commerce clause was, another weapon in the hands of those who wanted to protect property rights from the attacks of the reformers was perhaps more important. In the years immediately after the Civil War, the radical Republicans had pushed through three Constitutional amendments, part of whose purpose at least was to protect the Negro in the Southern states. The wording of one clause of the Fourteenth Amendment, however, had wider implications. 'Nor shall any state,' it read, 'deprive any person of life, liberty, or property, without due process of law.' The word 'person' was read, properly enough, to include the legal person or corporation. What gave the clause a larger importance than had probably been intended was the wide interpretation of the phrase 'due process of law'. This was read to mean not merely that proper legal procedures must be followed, but that judges were entitled to enquire whether legislation was reasonable both in its intentions and in its effects. The Justices of the Supreme Court could, if they chose, act as legislators. The due process clause brought state governments under the same sort of judicial restraint as the federal government had been subjected to the Constitution itself and so created important areas in which neither government could act. Mr Justice Harlan might have spoken for state acts also when he once declared that 'if we don't like an Act of Congress, we don't have much trouble to find grounds for declaring it unconstitutional'.

Such attitudes, however widespread and well established, were in no way inevitable. The intellectual attack which ultimately destroyed them was chiefly the work of two remarkable lawyers, both Justices of the Supreme Court. It is simpler to describe the younger first. Louis Brandeis, born in 1856, was appointed to the Court by President Wilson as late as 1916, but he had made a towering reputation as a crusading lawyer in labour and civil liberties cases long before that. A man with an enormous capacity for mastering and expounding complex data, it was he more than anyone who made respectable the appeal to social facts, rather than to mere precedent and general argument, in pleading a case. An even greater figure was Oliver Wendell Holmes, a Massachusetts aristocrat born in 1841 and appointed to the Court by Theodore Roosevelt in 1902. He sat for thirty years. Unlike Brandeis, Holmes was not a reformer, though during their years together on the Court they often saw eye to eye. What moved Holmes was the belief that his fellow judges too often imported into the law their own social prejudices, and that that was improper. He was neither for nor against big business, he was neither for nor against labour. He *was* in favour of free speech and social experiment, and he was not willing to see the

Fourteenth Amendment used vigorously to protect property rights, and only feebly to protect personal rights.

An adaptable democracy

Great as the power of Supreme Court Justices is, however, it rests in the end on public acquiescence. In time they usually modify their decisions to bring them into line with public opinion if it is sufficiently strongly held. As Mr Dooley put it, the Supreme Court 'follows th'iliction returns'. But when public opinion is sufficiently strongly held, party politicians of course also fall into line with it. It is for this reason that in American politics third parties seldom actually attain power. In normal times neither of the major parties has so strong an ideology as to prevent it from adapting to new, powerful pressures. Third parties are cut off just at the point where they are beginning to show signs of some success. In a sense, national parties exist only to capture the Presidency. Between elections, party discipline, as many a President has discovered to his cost, is very weak. Between elections, Senators and Congressmen weigh the national interest, so far as they discern it, against the interests of their states or districts. Their influence in Washington rests partly on their capacity to obstruct, and partly on their ability to co-operate. An American politician is a diplomat or negotiator far more than is a British politician. The attack on the trusts raised the whole question of what, if competition were once abandoned, should be put in its place. What form of regulation would be desirable? What form of regulation would be safe? What form of regulation would be moral? These were all questions about which the Progressives wrangled, pragmatists against ideologists. Such dialectic is not confined to Communists. If we ask what distinguished the Progressive movement from earlier reform movements, part of the answer may be as follows. Earlier Americans had demanded reforms chiefly as producers. They had wanted higher prices, or higher wages, or more opportunity. Now Americans were demanding reforms partly at least as consumers—consumers, that is, in the most general sense—consumers of a wide range of goods and services, some provided by the government, some merely regulated or guaranteed by the government, but which they could not provide for themselves. The task of a politician was to pick his way among conflicting interests and ideas, and the task became most complex for the man at the apex of the whole system—the President himself. It was to this task that Theodore Roosevelt had to address himself in 1901.

Left: *A suitable case for Progressive supervision—brokers at the curbside stock exchange in Broad Street, New York*

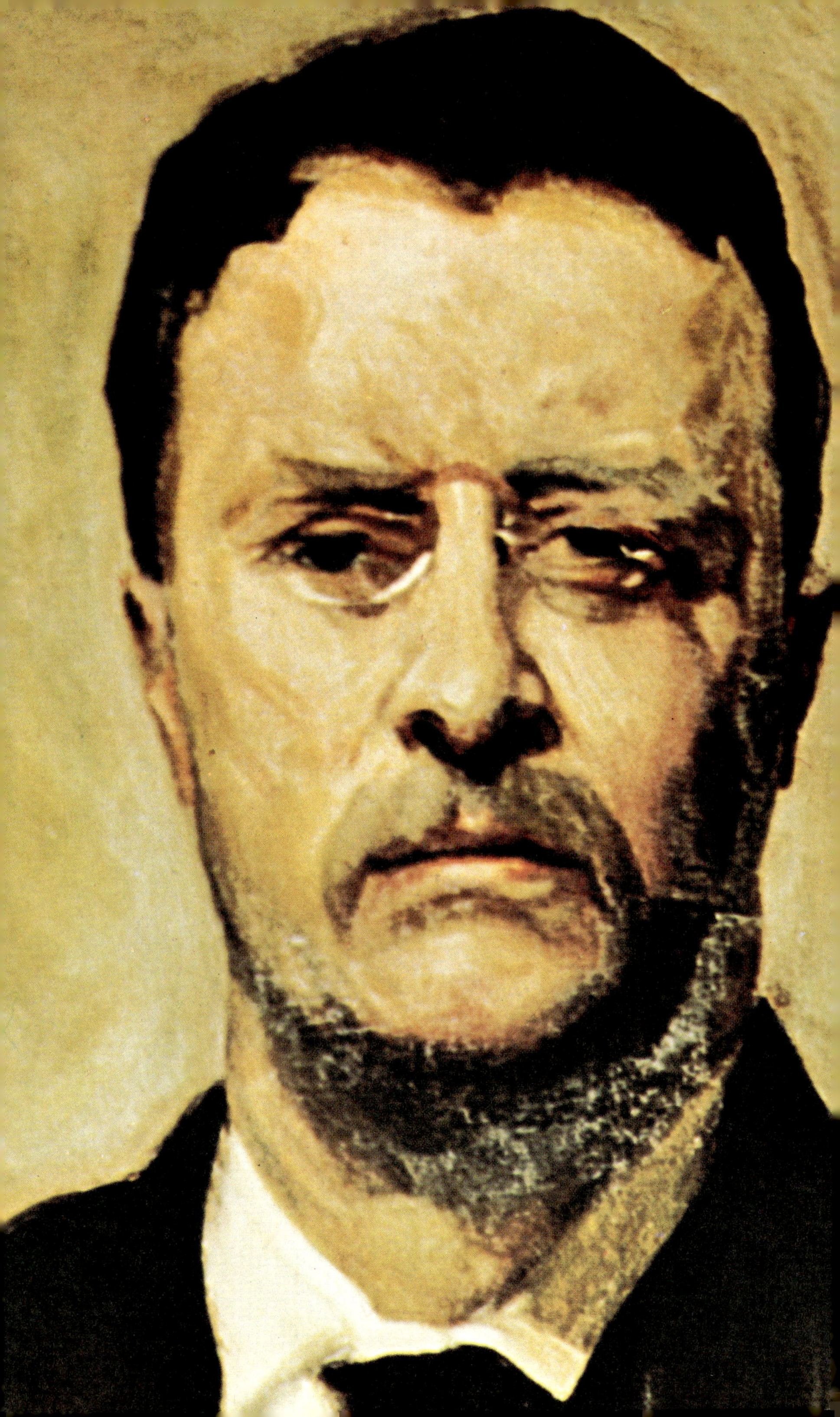

Chapter 5
The Positive President

Roosevelt did not spring up at once as the leader of a fully recognised Progressive movement. His position in 1901 was quite different. He had come to the presidency by accident; he had not won it in his own right. His political credit was less for that reason—nobody owed him anything. Moreover, the presidency was far from being the central office it has since become. Members of both houses of Congress cherished their independence, their leaders were powerful political figures, and the techniques of co-operation between the White House and Capitol Hill were primitive. Convention, indeed, forbade too close an intimacy. No President since Jefferson had addressed Congress in person, a convention not to be broken until Woodrow Wilson's time. And, while the President could propose and even draft legislation, the amount of direct support he could give to his proposals was not great.

The two houses of Congress were very different in character, more so than they have since become, and they maintained a lively rivalry, in which the Senate, unlike most other upper chambers, more than held its own. The members of the House of Representatives were chosen by direct popular elections; the members of the Senate were not. Until 1913, when a reform which was one of the last achievements of the Progressive movement changed the rule, they were elected by state legislatures. This had the effect—as the framers of the Constitution had intended—of removing the Senate from the influence of democracy, to some extent at least. It made it easier for powerful and wealthy men to find their way to the Senate without fighting their way up through the lower reaches of politics, and easier to stay there when they arrived. The politics of small groups is significantly different from the politics of large ones, and the Senate was a small group. It was also an undisciplined group. Presided over by the Vice-President, who was not a member, the Senate had a long tradition of egalitarianism. It was easy to frustrate business and hard to expedite it. A handful of leading and influential Senators

Left: *The statesman—Fred W.Wright's portrait in oils of TR*

ME
IND
S.C.
KAN
TEX
GA
N.H
K.Y.
MICH
N.Y.
N.J.
ILL
CAL
PA
MINN
VA
MASS
WIS
N.C.
LA
MISS
DEL

dominated the proceedings by agreement among themselves, and one gained influence by conforming to and manipulating the rules of this club. Senators were individualists more than party regulars. They were also generally deeply conservative. The conservatism of the Senate was a powerful obstacle to reform by legislation.

'Tsar' Reed and 'Uncle Joe'
The House of Representatives could hardly have been more different. Its membership was much larger, directly elected, and subject to re-election every two years. The business of the House would have fallen into chaos under rules as lax as those of the Senate. It was presided over by a Speaker, ordinarily chosen by the members of the majority party. The post-war period, during which major issues of principle were hard to find, paradoxically increased the pressure for party regularity, and two Speakers gave it institutional form. T.B.Reed of Maine – 'Tsar Reed' – formulated the rules which gave virtually autocratic power to the Speaker and to the chairmen of committees, who were also nominees of the majority party. When Reed retired from the Speakership and from the House of Representatives (on a point of conscience; he was unwilling to preside over a party which was committed, he believed, to imperialism), he was succeeded by Joseph Cannon – 'Uncle Joe' – of Illinois. Cannon, who held office as Speaker from 1901 to 1911, had even more power than Reed, and he used it more and more ruthlessly as his own highly conservative views became increasingly out of tune with his times. In 1910 a revolt in the House by a combination of Democrats and Radical Republicans deprived the Speaker of much of his power, and no Speaker since has achieved Cannon's importance. But, whether because Reed prized procedure and party regularity above all, or because Cannon was a cunning, ruthless conservative, the House in the first decade of the 20th century was not an easy body through which to pass reform measures. It was not by accident that the demand for reform of Congress came to rank high on many a Progressive list of reforms.

On Roosevelt's side it may be questioned how great his own faith in legislation was. In a country so various as the United States, the charge that any piece of legislation was 'special', in the sense that it benefited a certain group rather than the people or the nation as a whole, was easily made and damaging. It was a charge to which the Democratic Party had, perhaps, become more sensitive than the Republican, but in the years before Roose-

Left: *The party leader. In 1904 the Republicans nominated Roosevelt for a second term in the presidency by acclamation*

velt took office more of a President's time was taken in vetoing private bills than in constructing positive legislation. All his life Roosevelt was apt to place more faith in the co-operation of honest men than in legislative rules. At any rate it was clear to him that legislation could not be his first resort. First he had to win the confidence of Congressmen, or some power with which to impress them, or both.

Taming the tycoons
Roosevelt's claim to political stature rests on the speed with which he grasped the essence of presidential power, the ways in which it could be exploited, and the occasions on which it could be successfully used. One such occasion arose in 1902. The railway systems running out of Chicago across the Northwest had been steadily consolidated, until by 1900 they consisted of two great groups, one controlled by James J.Hill, with the support of John Pierpont Morgan, the other by E.H.Harriman. Hill and Harriman were among the greatest names in the railway world. Morgan was supreme in finance. A furious battle developed between the two groups for control of the entire system, a battle which ended in a compromise. All the railways would be brought together under a holding company – the Northern Securities Company – and the contestants would share control and profits.

In its nature this deal was no different from many that had taken place successfully in the past. What made it different, as Roosevelt grasped, was its scale, the size and reputation of the financial interests involved, and the fact that the public were particularly sensitive to railway mergers. It was Roosevelt's merit to see that the very scale of the merger made the parties involved more vulnerable, not less. There was in existence a law against such mergers – the so-called Sherman Act of 1890. It was a weak law, and it had largely fallen into disuse under Cleveland and McKinley. Roosevelt instructed his Attorney-General to bring an action against the Northern Securities Company, and when the case came before the Supreme Court he won a narrow victory. By a vote of five to four, the Justices decided against the company. (Justice Holmes wrote the minority opinion, the first of his famous dissents, and a promising friendship with Roosevelt came to an end.) The financial world was outraged, but the public applauded. It is doubtful whether the practical effect of this decision on the conduct of the railways was great. It is even doubtful whether that conduct had been particularly bad. Both Hill and Harriman, whatever their defects, were dedicated railway men, and Morgan personified the rigid, upright tradition of conventional banking. These men were not freebooters; they *were* too powerful. What Roosevelt accomplished, all he needed to accomplish, perhaps all he wanted to accomplish, was to demonstrate that trusts must take notice of the national interest, and that they could be held to account by a sufficiently active and courageous President.

Yet Roosevelt was not anxious to undertake suits. His real desire, increasingly so as he remained in office, was to control the trusts, not to break them up. He had a keen sense of the value to the country of the energy and skill of big businessmen. He did not fear or hate or even particularly distrust them. He believed that they needed control, and that they would yield to control only when they saw that they could do nothing else. It was above all the task of the President to make that plain. Yet when it was made plain, the practical business of devising means of control remained. Roosevelt's preferred means was the development of control commissions staffed by non-political experts. Here he reflected one element in the Progressive movement: the belief in scientific government. He believed that independent commissions, staffed by men who knew their jobs and were respected both by the public and by industrialists, would be the best means of controlling industry, and he did so because he believed that the experts would agree among themselves. The social scientist's belief that if you accumulate more facts they will lead open-minded men towards agreement was apparent here.

The scope of his legislative success shows the limitations which were still felt by most people to be important. He achieved passage of a law giving workmen's compensation to all government employees – but government employees were debarred from the right to strike, and so, it could be held, needed special protection. He pushed through a factory inspection law and a child labour law in the District of Columbia – but the nation's capital was a federal enclave in which laws could only be made by Congress; hence the law implied no enlargement of federal power. He obtained a law compelling the use of safety appliances on the railways – an exercise of federal control over interstate commerce which roused the public interest in a special way, for almost anyone might be a railway passenger.

Roosevelt found it hardest to achieve what he most wanted: the ability to intrude in the activity of major industries before they had done harm and not afterwards. His demand for legislation broke on the rock of Senate conservatism. His only resource was to continue with prosecution under the Sherman Act, sometimes with

Left: *TR meets Negro children in Summerville, South Carolina*

formal success, but not always with practical effect. Something, however, could be done when industry wanted the support of government. The railways, for example, were suffering from the ability of powerful customers to demand rebates on the rates for freighting their goods; so, of course, were the smaller customers with less bargaining power. With the support of many railway leaders, the Elkins Act of 1903, which forbade rebates, was passed. Though it was not very effective, it did something to show that the front of big business was not entirely solid, and so helped to allay public alarm. Moreover, when it was shown not to be effective it was made more so by the passage of the Hepburn Act of 1906. The passage of one act made the passage of the next easier.

There were limitations also in Roosevelt's own ideas of what was necessary. We should not attribute to him ideas that are more modern than his time. Although he was regarded as dangerously radical by conservatives in his day, he did not, for example, support the campaign led by Senator Beveridge for a national law governing the hours and conditions of child labour. Outrageous though the exploitation of child labour was, in this his instinct may have been sound. The various circumstances in which children were employed in different areas of the country at different stages of economic development would have made an effective, or even a just, national law almost impossible to draft.

On occasion the President had an opportunity for independent action. In 1902 a prolonged strike broke out in the anthracite mining region of Pennsylvania and the neighbouring states. The circumstances were almost as unfavourable to a settlement as were those of the British coal strike which brought on the General Strike of 1926. The mines were in the hands of many small owners, loosely held together in a variety of agreements with the railways that took their coal to East Coast markets, railways which themselves owned some of the mines. The miners had hitherto never been adequately organised, and when John Mitchell, the outstanding leader of the United Mineworkers of America, moved into the anthracite regions, the owners resisted strongly.

Roosevelt's strategy was to confer with both sides, and even to bring them together — not formally, for the owners would not admit Mitchell's right to speak for their employees, but under the guise of a fact-finding exercise. He succeeded in having the dispute turned over to an arbitration commission, which worked out a suitable compromise. There can be no doubt of Roosevelt's consid-

Right: *A thorn in the flesh of Progressives — House Speaker J.G.Cannon (foreground), caricatured as an omnipotent sultan*

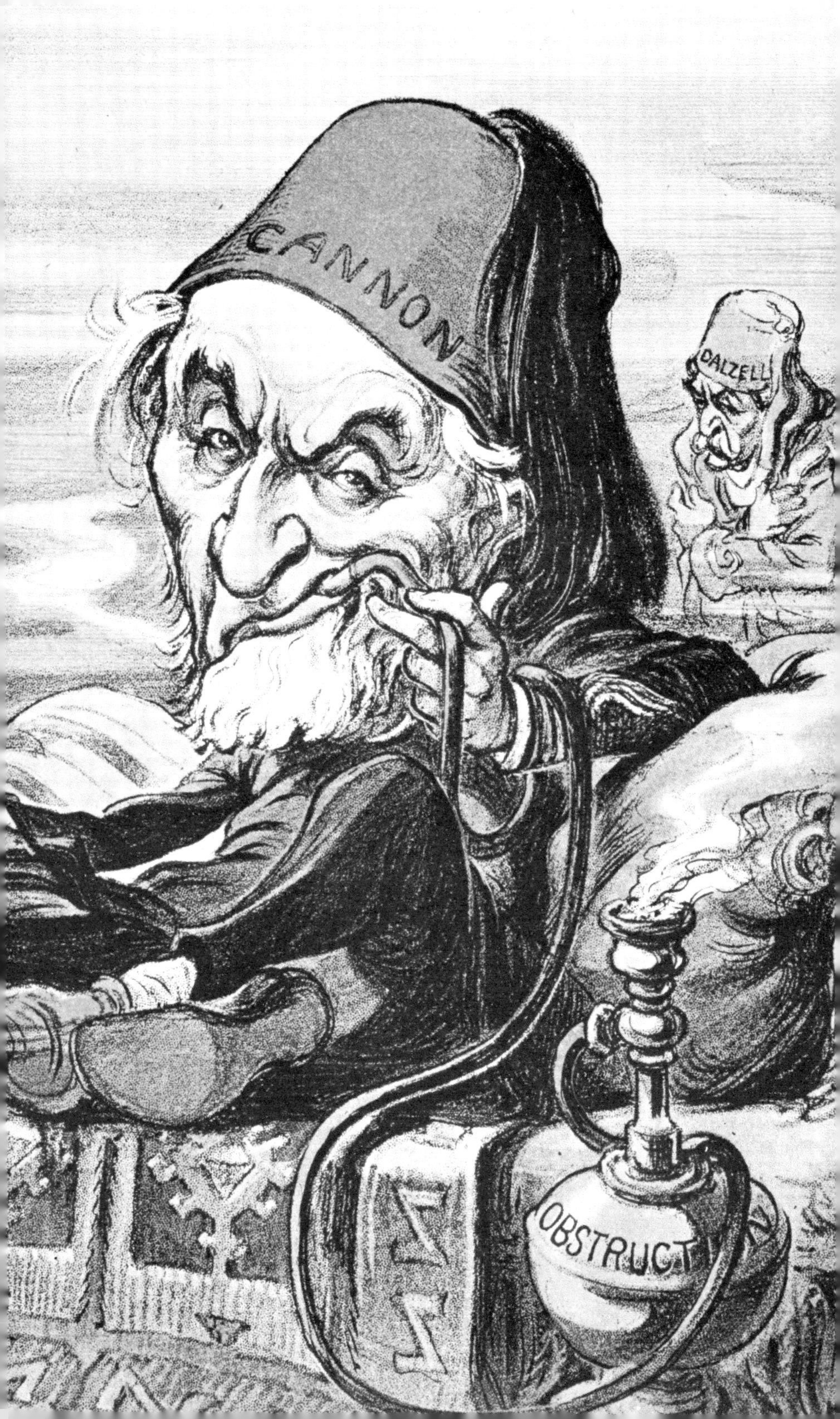
CANNON
DALZELL
OBSTRUCT

erable success. He gained the credit for ending the strike, he had set a useful if modest precedent for his preferred method of 'impartial' adjudication of industrial disputes, he had shown himself undaunted by 'big labour' as earlier by 'big business', and he had got across the image of himself as the guardian of the public interest, the effective spokesman of the whole nation. The identification of Roosevelt with the cause of national unity had been enhanced.

The sense of national unity both as essential for itself and as essential if many other purposes were to be achieved, was central to much Progressive thinking. No doubt a defensive element played an important part. If action were not taken quickly, certain possibilities would be closed for ever. This was a cry which rallied a larger body of support than any single reform could do. In no area was it more effective than in one with which Roosevelt's name is especially connected — conservation. At the end of the 19th century, men first became conscious that the natural resources of the United States were not inexhaustible, and also that there were rival demands on them. At that time the most obvious problems were those of water and forests. As early as 1873 the American Association for the Advancement of Science had drawn attention to the squandering of forest land. In 1891 the Forest Reserve Act was passed, which authorised the President to set aside public forest land as not for sale. Some forty-five million acres of land were withdrawn by Harrison, Cleveland, and McKinley. Roosevelt withdrew 150 million acres, and added another eighty-five million in Alaska and the Northwest, withdrawn until their resources had been surveyed by the government. Equally important, he had the national forests transferred from the Department of the Interior to the Department of Agriculture, where the Forest Bureau, under the father of modern conservation, Gifford Pinchot, administered them on scientific lines. Here, as so often, Roosevelt's chief contribution was to give encouragement and publicity and effective support to men already active in the field. If public concern had not already existed he could have done nothing. But he could and did tip the balance against exploitation and in favour of conservation. His successors were to show how the movement could flag lacking that steady support from the man at the heart of government.

Water was perhaps a more tricky problem even than forests. Much of the timber land of the country had fallen into the hands of big lumber companies. These had little

Right: *'Elisha' Roosevelt sets the bears of the Inter-State Commerce Commission on the bad boys of Wall Street (1907)*

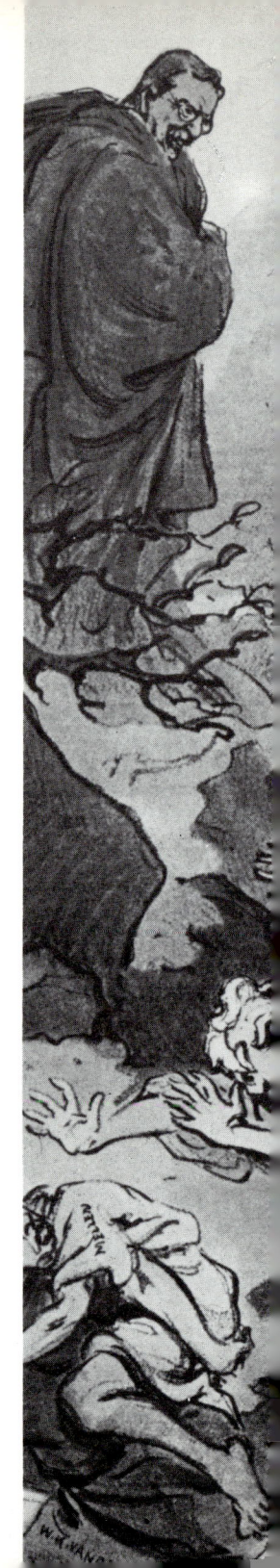

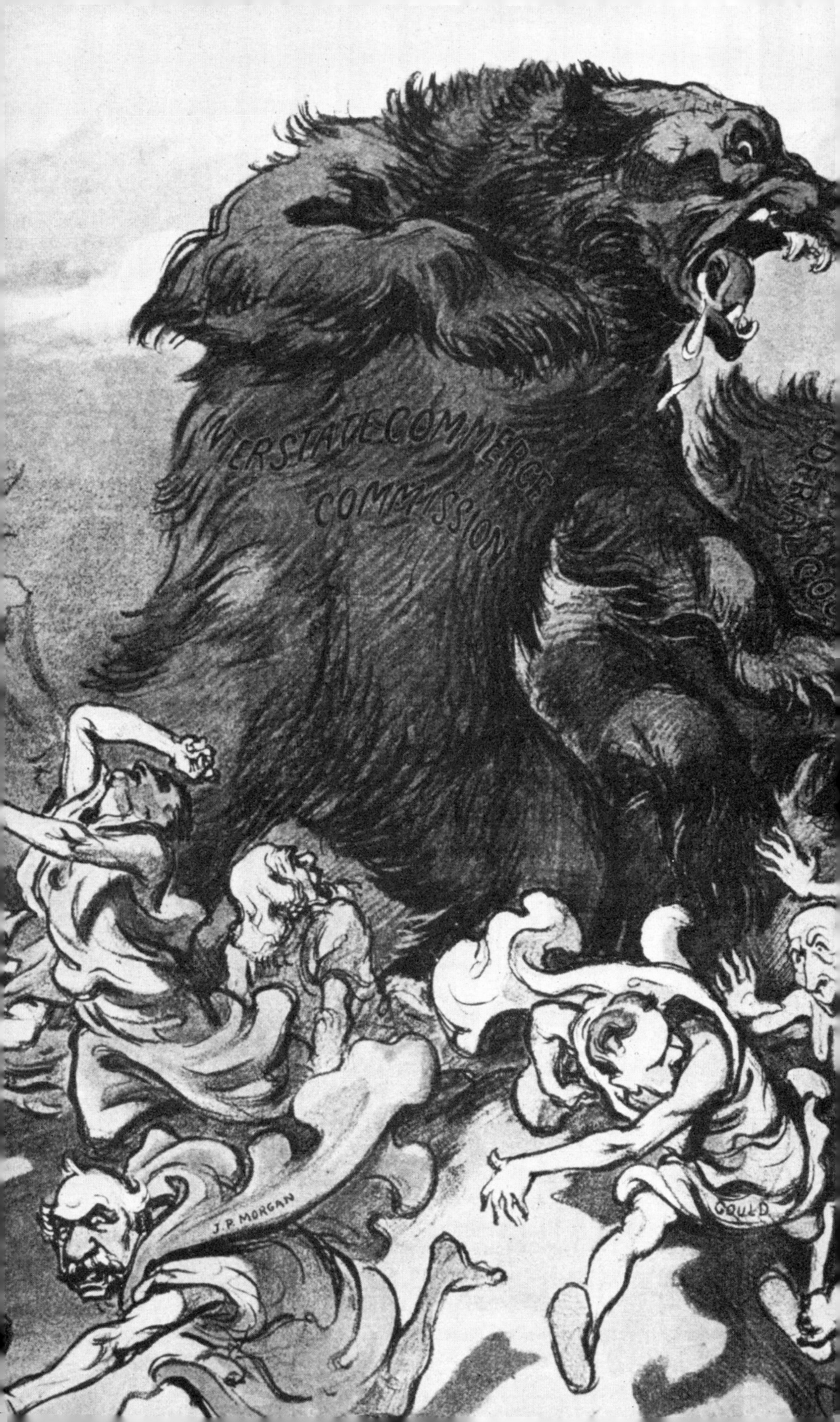
ERSTATECOMMERCE
COMMISSION
J.P. MORGAN
GOULD

concern for national amenities, but out of concern for their own livelihood they had some regard for replanting where they felled. Lumber companies become scientific foresters out of mere self-interest. Farmers are less farsighted. By the time the conservation movement became effective, much permanent damage had been done to arid regions. It was in the West that the need for control was greatest; but the West was also the home of intransigent individualism. Fortunately, this was a matter where different interests worked against each other, and so a matter in which Roosevelt could intervene. For example, cattle men, who deeply distrusted government intervention to restrict their use of grazing land, needed government help with their water problems. The Carey Land Act of 1894 had been the first attempt to deal with the problem. It allowed states in desert areas to sell land for purposes of reclamation and irrigation; but the act only succeeded in demonstrating that this was a problem too large for private enterprise. Roosevelt took the next step in pushing the Reclamation Act of 1902, which provided that irrigation should be paid for by the proceeds of public land sales, and that it should be under federal government control. The great dams of the American West, supplying and controlling water for several states, were built under this act. At the same time Roosevelt was active in the establishment of a whole range of national parks and nature reserves. But perhaps most important in this field of activity was that he set up the government machinery—the bureaux within the Departments of Agriculture and the Interior—which could be used and developed by his successors.

Foreign policy is by its nature the President's preserve and it was one in which Roosevelt took a lively interest. Certainly treaties with foreign powers must be approved by the Senate, and so become a matter of party politics, as, notoriously, Woodrow Wilson discovered in the fight over the Treaty of Versailles; but not all foreign policy is a matter of treaties. We shall deal in greater depth with foreign affairs in a later chapter. Here it is worth noting that the international position of the United States was still one of such security that the President, in many respects, had large scope for activity—or, of course, inactivity. It was because his predecessors had become so inactive that Theodore Roosevelt was able to make so much of a mark in foreign affairs. In the Western hemisphere, shrewdly judging that there would be no effective European reaction, he acted strongly, largely at the expense of Britain and Canada, even while he protested—sincerely no doubt—his devotion to the idea of Anglo-Saxon solidarity. He pushed through the acquisition of the Panama Canal Zone by the United States, and set in hand the building of the canal; but he also insisted that it should be American-controlled, and that Britain should relinquish any share in its control.

Elsewhere his activities were more circumscribed, but just because the United States was yet seen to be remote from international politics, the President's role as a mediator and arbitrator could be enlarged. What could be done to enlarge it, Roosevelt did. At the end of the Russo-Japanese War he invited the two countries to conduct their negotiations in the United States, he was lavish with advice to both, and he took much credit for the Treaty of Portsmouth, New Hampshire, which finally ended the war. When an international crisis developed over Morocco in 1905, he sent a delegation to the conference that settled the quarrel — as he was entitled to do but need not have done — and his influence with the German Kaiser contributed to a peaceful outcome. In all this, active though he was, Roosevelt was taking no risk for his country. The United States was put neither to danger, nor to expense. What was at risk was Roosevelt's reputation and that of his office, and these he succeeded in protecting and enhancing.

The charge most often brought against Roosevelt is that his successes were not real. They were merely in the field of public relations. They left nothing behind. Still further, Roosevelt was interested in public relations more than in accomplishment. For all his vigorous speeches, he seldom committed himself to a battle not easily won. There is something in the charges, but it may be that what the American people most wanted then was not change, but a voice in the world; and a voice Roosevelt gave them.

In his day the convention established by George Washington that a President may not hold office for more than two terms, was still only a convention. It remained a convention until Franklin Roosevelt broke it; but was so powerful a convention that Theodore Roosevelt did not even consider breaking it, although his first term had been incomplete and not won by election. Inevitably, therefore, he suffered the decline of power that afflicts presidents when their tenure is known to be nearly over. But his departure from office in 1909 was welcomed by conservatives with a sense of relief. That single fact perhaps defines his stature as a reformer.

Left, top: *Swiss cartoon shows 'Hercules' Roosevelt dominating the wild bull of anarchism. But there were failures too.*
Bottom: *'Hamlet' Roosevelt mourns his inability to revise the tariff: 'Thus the tariff doth make cowards of us all'*

The Shape of Things to Come

Many features of the contemporary American scene had their beginnings in the age of Roosevelt. Edison's kinetescope pictures were first given a public showing in 1894. But not until 1902 was the first theatre devoted entirely to motion pictures opened. Many early movie houses concentrated on providing newsreels of current events, like the Tacoma, Washington theatre with its newsreels of the Boer War **(right, top)**. And after the movies—a visit to the soda fountain. The sale of such soft drinks as Coca-Cola **(below)** rose dramatically during the early years of the 20th century. But the most significant social and economic development during the Roosevelt era was the mass-production of motor cars **(right, bottom)**. Spearheaded by Henry Ford's works in Detroit, in 1908 the industry manufactured over 60,000 cars, and there were nearly 200,000 automobiles on American roads. Ten years later there were to be more than five-and-a-half million

ADMISSION
10¢
EDISON'S
MOVING
PICTURES
MOVING PICTURES
Armored Troop Train Crossing
MODDER RIVER S.A.
COAL TRUCKS LOADED with
BRITISH SOLDIERS
SCENES
OF INTEREST In the
SOUTH AFRICA.

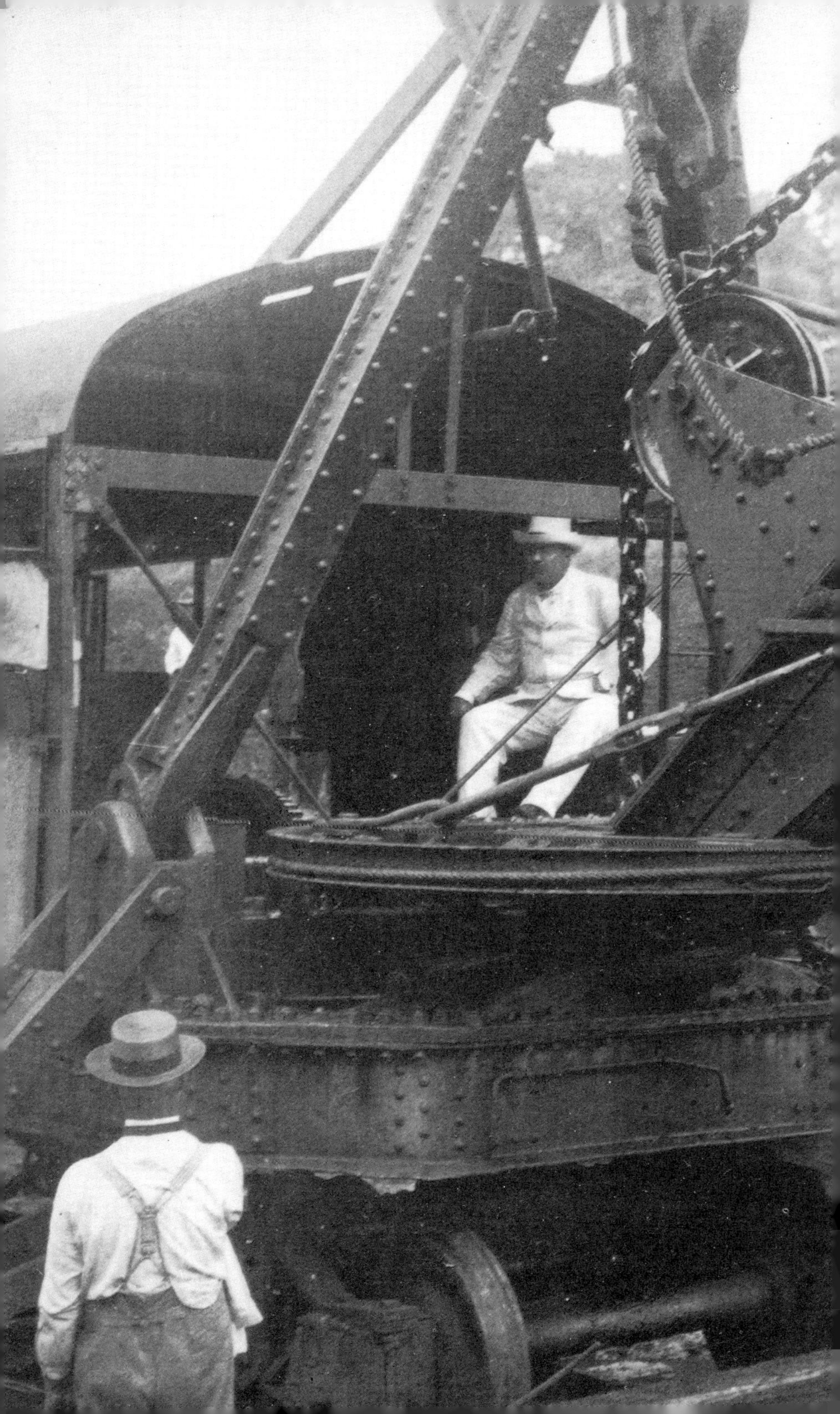

Chapter 6
America and the World

Throughout most of the 19th century Americans gave little thought to foreign affairs. The War of Independence itself had been in large part a struggle for freedom from involvement in the quarrels of Europe. After it was won, the events of the 19th century seemed to confirm that non-involvement with Europe was the right course. The United States quickly became beyond question the most powerful state in her own hemisphere, north or south. Certainly, through much of the century she was still weak by the standards of the European powers; but she was protected both by the Atlantic Ocean and by European rivalries. Though she was too weak to constitute a threat to the great powers, she was too powerful to be worth attacking, and powerful enough to be worth conciliating. On their side, Americans had no strong reason to intervene in world affairs. They had a continent to develop. Their growth in population and economic strength, apparent both to themselves and to others, meant that they could always postpone intervention and, with the passage of time, always be better placed to intervene. Still more, the growth of the sectional rivalry which ended in civil war meant that Americans found it hard to agree on a foreign policy. Any policy, in foreign affairs as in domestic, seemed likely to benefit one section more than the other. Inaction had attractions.

None of this meant, of course, that America withdrew from the world as, say, Japan had done for much of the century. Americans travelled where they chose, traded where they chose, invested where they chose, settled where they chose. They took a full part in the affairs of the world as individuals, but they did so without supposing that their government needed an international policy. Enjoying what one American historian has termed 'free security', they also supposed that the world would advance in civilisation – the common 19th-century liberal belief. America's part in the advance of mankind was to set an example, not to exert power. None of this conflicted

Left: Teddy ('I took Panama') Roosevelt rides a steam-shovel during the construction of the great canal in 1906

93

with an aggressive policy of expansion and exploitation on the American continent. It meant only that the question of relations with other states could be and was postponed, and with it the question of what American policy should be when the continent was at last fully settled, as none doubted that eventually it would be. There were a few men of more active vision. Chief among them, perhaps, was William Henry Seward, Lincoln's Secretary of State, who bought Alaska from Russia in 1867, and had the utmost difficulty in persuading Congress to meet the trifling cost of 7,200,000 dollars.

The end of the century changed all that. The event which brought the United States forcibly to world consciousness was the Spanish-American War of 1898. Spanish control over the remnants of her empire had been weakening. Especially in Cuba her rule was incompetent, corrupt, and expensive. Sporadic rebellion had broken out, which the Spaniards found increasingly difficult to put down. Continuous fighting ruined the sugar crop, which was the island's chief staple, most of which was bought by the United States. Famine brought disease, which threatened to spread to the United States. And a stream of miserable refugees arrived in the United States, spreading word of Spanish atrocities and urging American intervention. Increasingly Americans came to the conviction that unless Spain could restore stable and civilised rule in the islands, she must be made to give them up. On their side, the Spaniards maintained that only the hope of American intervention was keeping the rebellion alive and that by refusing to denounce it Americans were themselves largely responsible for those evils which they did denounce.

The conquerors
Between views so opposed no compromise was possible. The end came when the American battleship *Maine*, on an ill-advised courtesy visit to Havana harbour, blew up and sank with heavy loss of life. The causes of the explosion have never been finally ascertained. Though the Spaniards denied responsibility and offered all the retribution they could, the United States forced the issue into war. So unevenly matched were the combatants that there could be no doubt where responsibility for the war lay, nor any doubt of its outcome. Nevertheless, the United States Army had decayed almost to nothing since the Civil War. A scratch force was hurriedly put together for the invasion of Cuba, largely composed of volunteer recruits. It succeeded in defeating the Spanish forces with surprising ease. The American navy was in better shape, and defeated the decrepit squadrons of Spain even more easily. Most importantly for the future, an Ameri-

can squadron under Commodore Dewey sought out and destroyed the Spanish Far Eastern fleet in Manilla harbour in the Philippines.

Beyond question the United States entered the war for largely altruistic and humanitarian reasons. The object was to free Cuba, not to take it over. That object was not betrayed. An undertaking not to acquire Cuba was written into the Congressional resolution which began the war. Cuba lies uncomfortably close to the United States, but whatever forms of interference the United States may have adopted in the island, then or later, formal control has not been one of them. The Philippines were another matter. Before the war began few Americans had given them any consideration. As Mr Dooley remarked, they hardly knew whether the Philippines were islands or canned fruit! Yet when the peace conference met it was fairly quickly – and to the surprise of Spain – determined that the Americans intended to keep them, paying for them certainly, but keeping them none the less. At about the same time, the United States took over Hawaii, where a republican government dominated by American settlers had recently overthrown the native queen and asked for accession to the United States. Denying herself Cuba, which had often in the past seemed bound to fall to her, the United States had managed to acquire an island empire which extended to the very edge of Asia.

The justification for taking and keeping the Philippines was that they could not simply be handed back to Spain, which was as incompetent to administer them as she had been to run Cuba. Nor could they be given independence, for they would not be allowed to keep it. Denied American protection, they would certainly be taken over by some predatory power – Germany, Britain, or Japan. Yet rather than see the islands fall into the hands of their rivals, all these powers preferred that the United States should have them. America was, so to say, everyone's second choice. The third possibility, that the United States might give the islands independence under some sort of guarantee which would protect them against third powers, was unattractive. It would mean less than full independence for the Philippines, and responsibility without power for the United States.

Yet Americans had doubts about the venture. The United States, republican and democratic, had, after all, won her own independence from an earlier empire. How could she now acquire an empire of her own? Most of the doubts were on behalf of the United States, rather than of the Philippines. Few Americans doubted that if the

Left: *TR's Florentine 'double'. Lively interventions in foreign affairs made President Roosevelt an international celebrity*

95

Philippines had to be controlled by a foreign power, it was best for them that that power should be the United States. They may well have been right. But what would be the effect on America herself of acquiring an empire? Could democratic, egalitarian institutions survive in the United States when the machinery for ruling an empire was set up? Would not the United States develop the large armed forces, the bureaucracy, the enhanced executive power, which were the marks of imperial states? And, equally serious, would not the commitment to defend an empire draw the nation into the quarrels of Europe, and deny her that freedom of decision which had been so valuable for one hundred years?

On the first point it can be quickly said that the fears proved exaggerated. The American empire was never big enough or important enough to make much mark on American domestic politics. The imperial civil service, the imperial army, did not develop; the increase in presidential power was barely noticeable. Whatever defects may have appeared in American domestic government, they had domestic causes, and were not made more difficult to solve by imperial complications. The second point calls for more consideration. Though the war to free Cuba was undertaken for idealistic reasons, and though the Philippines were acquired without adequate consideration of the implications, American imperialism did not appear out of the blue. There had been indications before the 1890s that some Americans at least wanted a more active foreign policy and thought the country needed it. Such a policy, of course, did not inevitably mean imperialism, but, hesitant and relatively insignificant as it was, American imperialism can best be understood as one response to a world situation which seemed threatening. More than most countries, the United States engaged in international affairs responsively. Her preference, like that of Britain, would have been the continuance of mid-19th-century world stability.

Economic stakes
Economic interests also played a part in the development of an outward-looking foreign policy. Even before 1890, but especially after the depression that began in 1893, there had been anxiety about the state of the American economy. Some observers felt that there was a danger of permanent over-production, with the unemployment and social unrest which would inevitably follow. An increase in state control to deal with this problem seemed undesirable to men trained in 19th-century liberalism. The other apparent answer was access to growing world

Right: A 1907 dig at TR's ambition to be a great President

Second
Second
First in War, First in
First in the heart
of his
NOBEL PRIZE
THE BIG STICK
CHASSMAN
ALONE IN CUBA

markets. America, it seemed, was bound to become more and more dependent on world trade. Yet the United States was not well equipped to protect her share of world trade. Her merchant marine was small, having fallen back sharply from the days when wooden sailing ships were dominant. A demand for a subsidised merchant ship programme arose—evidence, if evidence is needed, that Americans are not slow to demand government help when they think it profitable. But if the American merchant fleet were to grow it would be helpless without a navy to protect it. The navy also must be enlarged.

There was another reason for enlarging the navy—the protection of the United States itself. Though the potential power of the United States was doubted by none and least of all by Americans, her actual power formed a ridiculous contrast with that of even many small South American states. Fear of what even the Chilean navy might accomplish if it appeared off the coast and bombarded American cities was real. A navy for coast defence was needed. Here were two contrasting requirements— large, heavily-armed ships to beat off an attack on American coasts, and fast, long-range ships as protection vessels. Fortunately the dominant naval theory of the day came to the rescue. This held that what a naval power needed was a battle fleet capable of defeating the enemy's fleet. Given that, commerce protection and coast defence alike would look after themselves. There might be some losses of merchant ships at sea, but not enough—at a time when the submarine was not yet a threat—to effect the outcome of a war. If that were true for Britain—where the theory gained its most influential support—it was still more true for the United States. The Americans set about the creation of a battle fleet.

At that time, when most vessels were still coal-burning, and when the range of coal-burning vessels, though increasing, was not very large, a fleet implied the possession of secure coaling stations, suitably placed. Island imperialism could be seen as a strategic necessity. At once the question of foreign policy was raised. To prevent foreign powers from acquiring bases in the Western hemisphere was obvious; and it was no more than a trifling extension of the old-established American doctrine, enunciated by President Monroe in 1823, that the Western hemisphere was not open for colonisation. Hardly more of a departure was the determination, quickly reached and enunciated, that if any canal were to be built linking the Atlantic and Pacific Oceans, it must be firmly under American control. Britain was persuaded to relinquish her established right to a share in the control

Right: *Joining the oceans—Lie's painting of the Panama Canal*

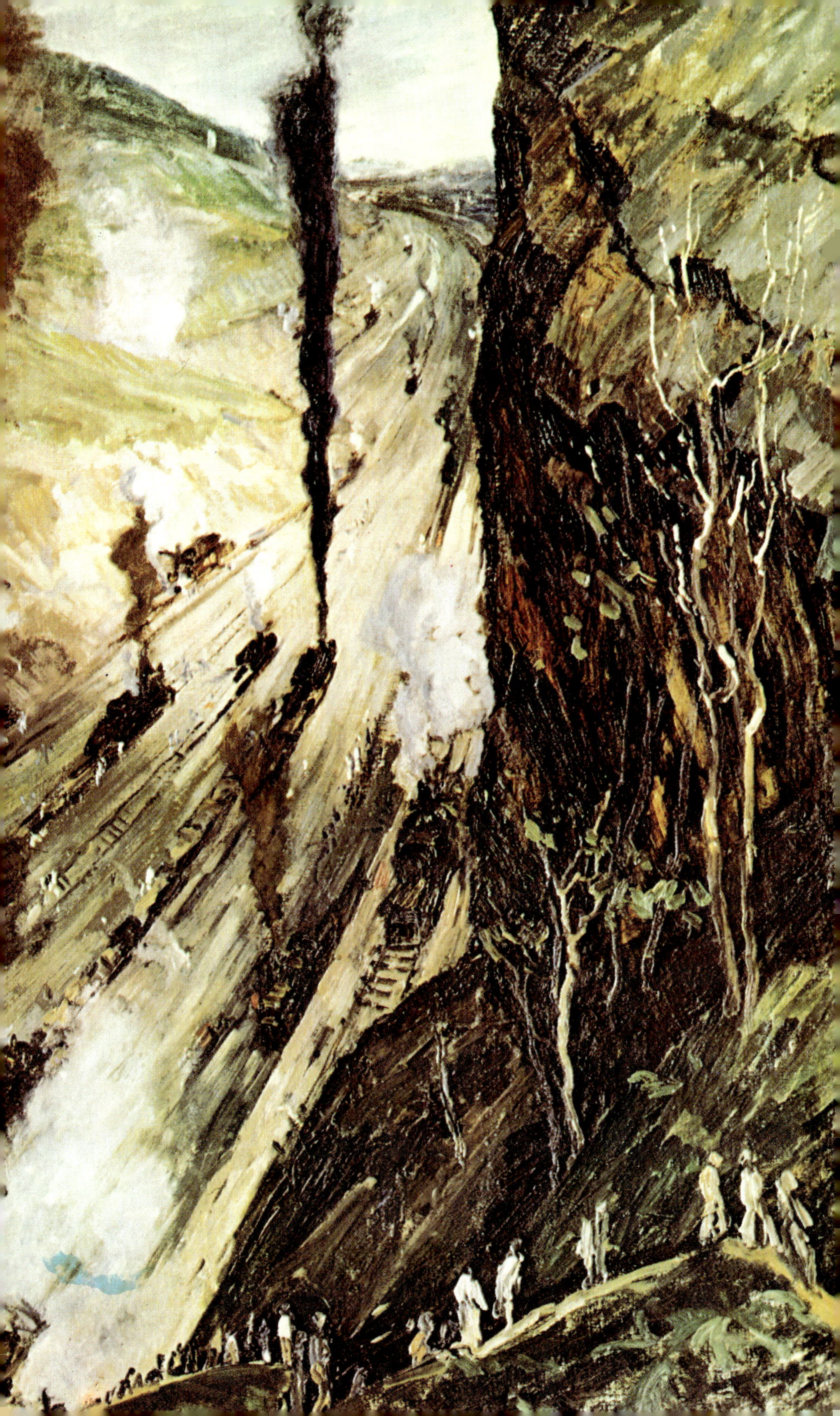

of such a canal, deriving from an Anglo-American treaty of 1850, and, after several different routes had been canvassed, the Canal Zone was taken over from the new republic of Panama and the Panama Canal was built.

When the Atlantic and Pacific were joined by the canal, the contrast between the two oceans as fields for American policy became apparent. The Atlantic offered no bases. As before, if the United States chose to remain aloof from Europe, the Atlantic formed a barrier which would-be attackers had to overcome; if she became involved in Europe, the Atlantic formed an obstacle to rapid and effective American action. But in the Pacific the position was different. The United States had acquired a chain of bases stretching across the ocean and ending in the Philippines. There was another significant difference. Europe was then the home of nearly all the world's great powers. American involvement in Europe would be not only difficult, but possibly costly as well. In Asia, on the other hand, the United States acted from the same position as Britain, or Germany, or France — powers which also had to act far from their home bases.

Far Eastern threat

The exception to this generalisation was provided by Russia, whose territory extended across to the Far East. Sea power could hardly be effective against Russia. But of more immediate interest was the position of Japan, the only Asiatic state with pretensions to being a great power. In American-Japanese relations, the acquisition of the Philippines posed a problem which was to become more and more apparent. Any American fleet strong enough to guard the Philippines against Japan would be strong enough to threaten Japan itself. Any Japanese fleet strong enough to protect Japan would, by that fact, have the Philippines as a hostage.

While Russia was the expansive, aggressive power in the Far East, any conflict between Japan and the United States remained latent. Even after the Japanese had been victorious in the Russo-Japanese war of 1903-04, there was no immediate occasion for conflict. The Japanese were, for the time being, exhausted by their efforts and, though enlarging their claims in Korea and Manchuria, showed no disposition to threaten acceptable standards of international behaviour. On his side, Theodore Roosevelt, while President, showed himself aware of the danger, and was not inclined to oppose what he saw as legitimate and direct Japanese interests in Asia; and his successors followed him in that policy, partly for his reasons and partly because they were increasingly concerned with other problems nearer home.

Initially too, Japanese ambitions were not directed

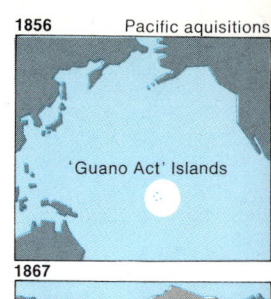

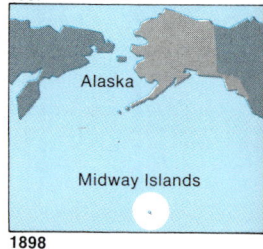

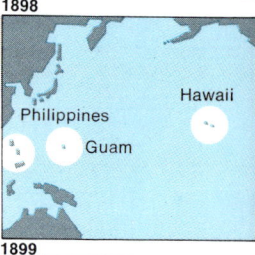

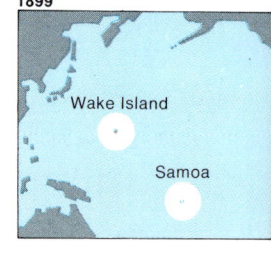

Pacific aquisitions

1856 'Guano Act' Islands

1867 Alaska / Midway Islands

1898 Philippines / Guam / Hawaii

1899 Wake Island / Samoa

Overseas expansion

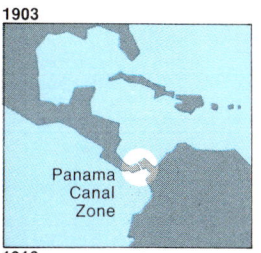

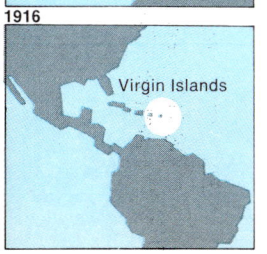

1898 Atlantic aquisitions
Puerto Rico

1903
Panama Canal Zone

1916
Virgin Islands

against China proper, and in Manchuria they showed no desire to interfere with American mission work. It was China, of course, which made the Far East a centre of world concern. The vast, ramshackle empire was still unified; but it was backward, it seemed incapable of reform, and it was doubtful how long it could remain united. The 'break-up of China' was in everyone's mind. It was generally supposed that Russia was eager for it to take place, so that she could enlarge her Asian dominion still further. If it did take place — and few were confident that it would not — the other powers were eager to ensure that they gained something from the wreck. But, on the whole, because the outcome of China's break-up was hard to predict, they wanted to stave it off as long as possible. The best evidence is provided by the outbreak of the Boxer Rising in 1900. All the powers sent contingents of troops to Peking to protect their nationals and to put down the rising; but when that was done, they were all, with the exception of the Russians, ready to withdraw. That was not mere altruism. All the powers calculated that their chances of gain would be greater if their rivals' forces were elsewhere.

The 'open door'

The United States took a leading part in advocating the maintenance of China and a policy of equal rights for all the powers with a foothold in the empire — the policy usually called the 'open door'. John Hay, Secretary of State, wrote circular letters to the powers asking their mutual agreement to the maintenance of China's integrity and to equal trading rights for all. All the powers gave their agreement in some form, though the Russian acceptance in particular was so hedged with qualifications as to be meaningless. But so far as Hay's policy was successful, it was because the powers had no immediate interest in destroying China, and not because American force stood behind it. Although the American navy had been built up to an impressive level, there is no evidence that American opinion would have supported a war for China against any European power or group of powers, and some evidence that it would not. The powers stalemated each other. In such circumstances, American preferences were given some weight, even though the United States refused to join any power in formal undertakings.

If American policy was negative and defensive in the Far East, it was still more so in European affairs. When the attention of the European powers shifted away **106 ▷**

Left: 'Imperial America'. **Next page:** *The 'great white fleet' of the US Navy passes through San Francisco Bay. To stress US maritime power, the fleet sailed round the world in 1907*

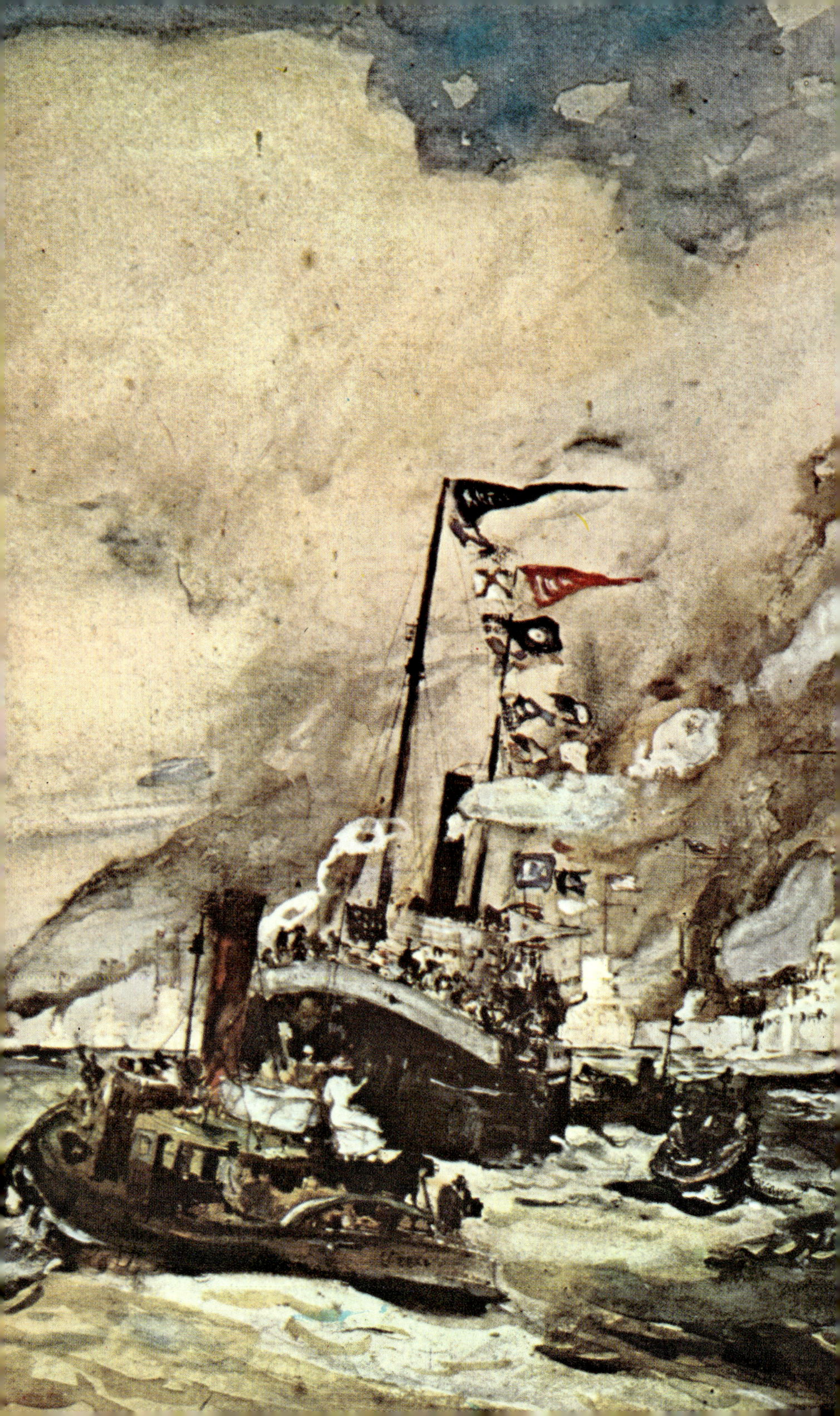

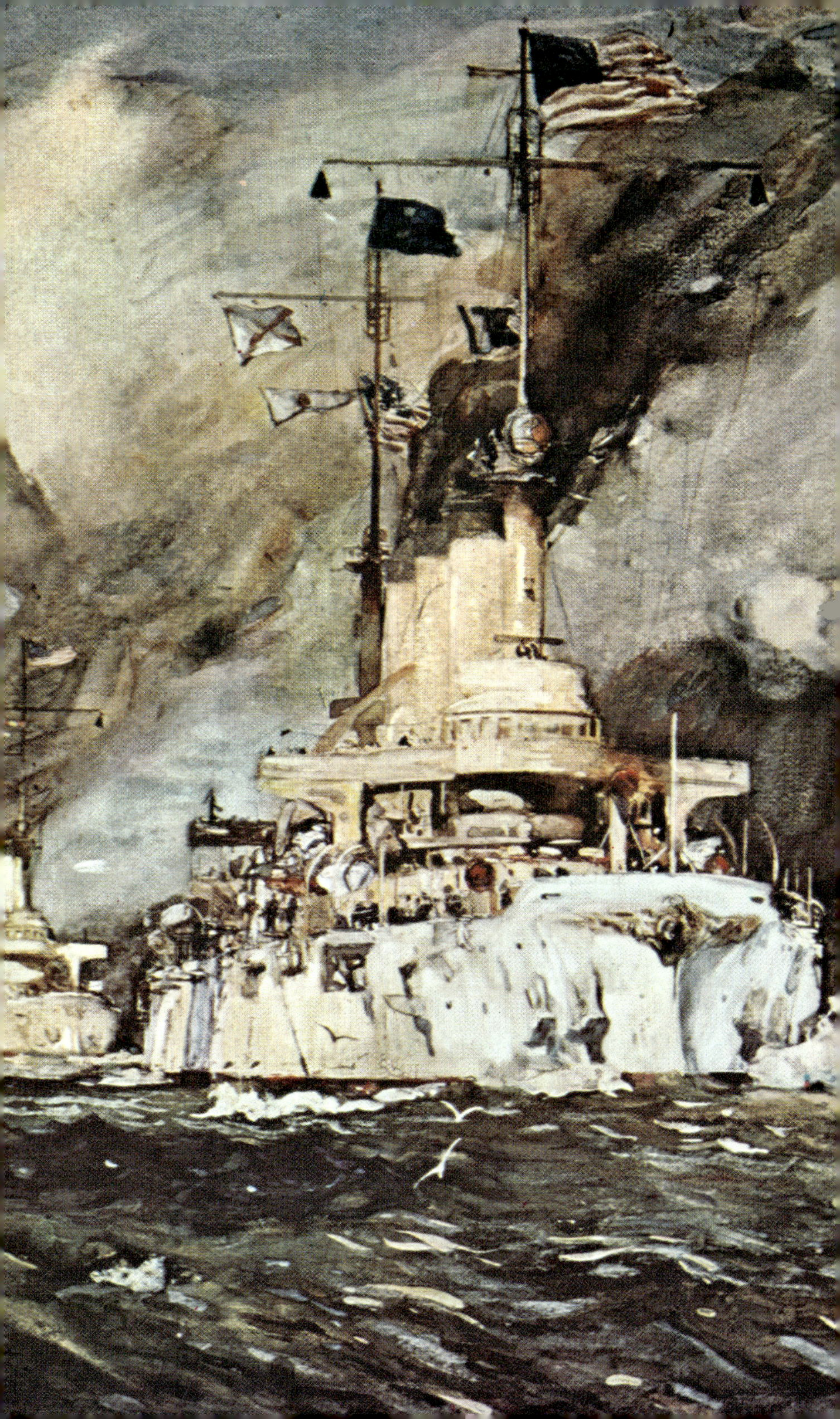

The Star-Spangled Empire

After several decades of relative indifference to the outside world, America burst upon the international scene at the end of the 19th century with her victory over the decrepit empire of Spain. The US Army took Cuba; the US Navy crushed the Spanish fleet at Manila Bay, 1st May 1898 **(right, top)**. But this striking assertion of the republic's military power was not welcomed by all Americans. Many despised what they saw as an unholy alliance between aggressive warmongering and infantile patriotism **(below)**. In particular, many feared that the United States, which had been born as a rebellious limb of the British Empire, was about to betray her heritage and herself become a great imperialist power. These fears were partly realised. America took over certain territories from the now-defunct Spanish Empire. And in Latin America, her 'natural' sphere of influence, the United States established a hegemony which was almost imperial in scope **(right, bottom)**

OUR EXPANSIVE UNCLE.
BUT IT'S ONLY TEMPORARY.

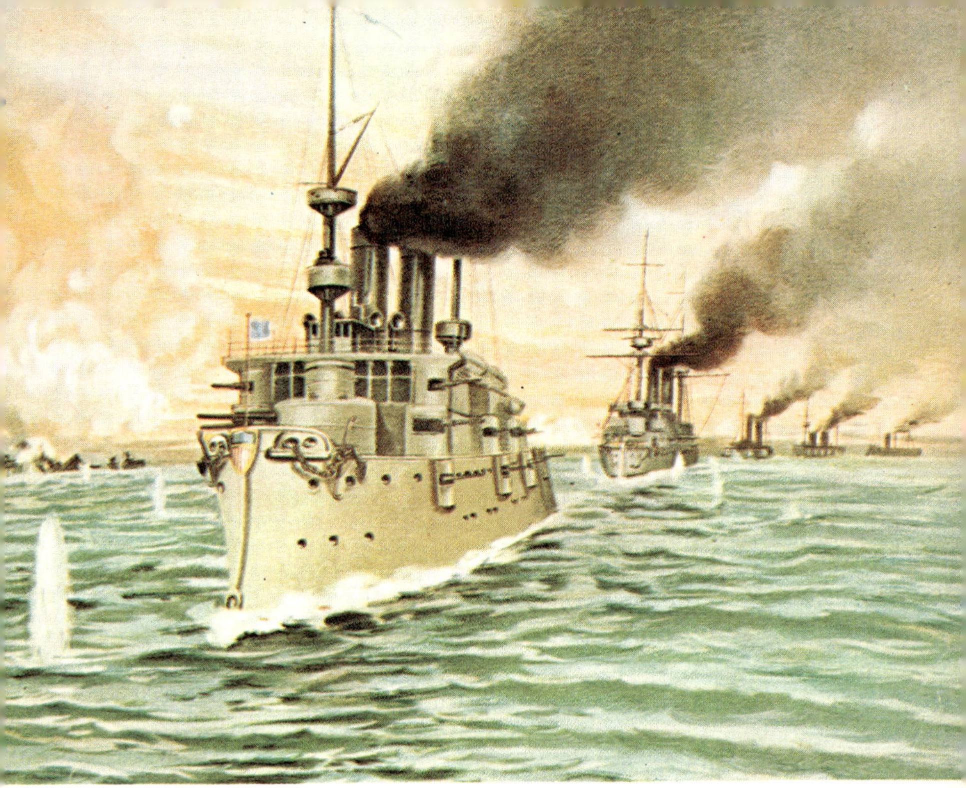

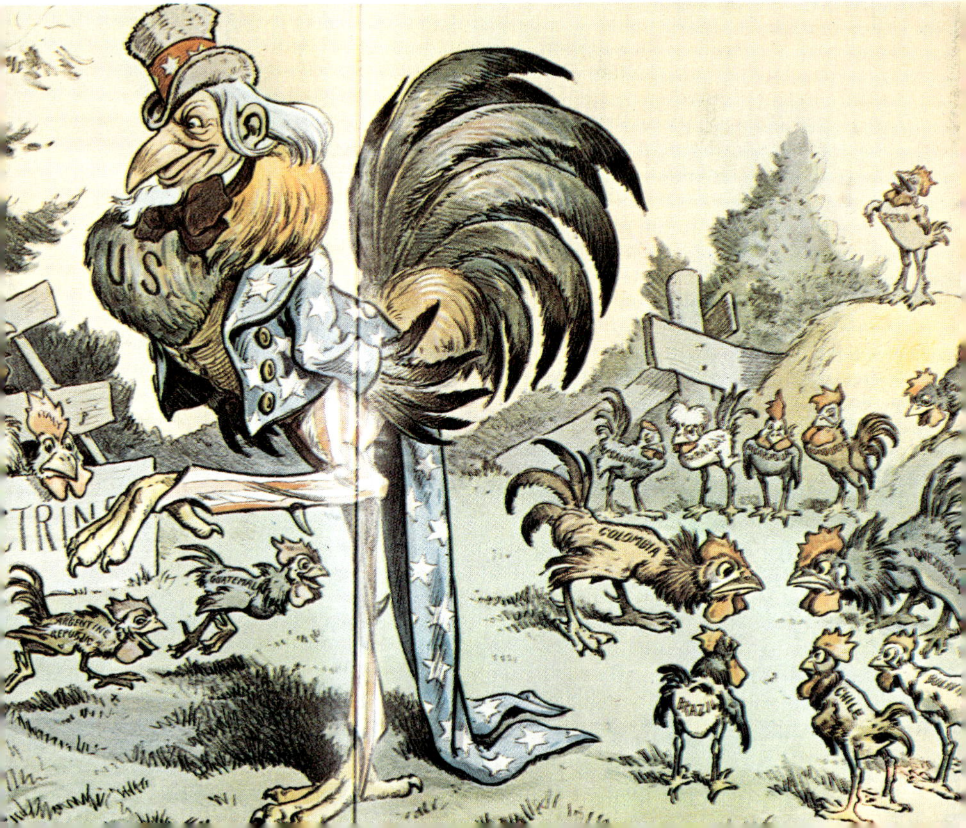

U S
TRIN
ARGENTINE REPUBLIC
COLOMBIA
BRAZIL
CHILE

from the Far East to Europe in the years immediately before the First World War, the American response was to sink back into isolationism. Most Americans watched the onset of the war with dismay but without feeling that there was anything useful they could do to stop it. They were far from certain where right lay in the quarrels that brought the war about. In a very traditional American way, they were disposed to blame the powers of the old continent almost equally. All were tainted with feudalism, militarism, dynastic rivalries, and other ancient evils from which the United States was happily free. Morality therefore gave no clear lead in determining which side the United States should support. On the other hand it was generally supposed in the early stages of the war that the United States had the power to protect her own interests and to enforce respect for them from all belligerents. Self-interest as well as morality thus suggested neutrality. Equally important, Americans had very various European backgrounds, and most still felt some sympathy for their country of origin. The German-Americans notably did so, while the Irish-Americans had reasons of their own for opposing Britain. Americans of Russian background were generally refugees with small love for the rulers of their empire. This variety of origin meant that any policy of support for one side or the other would have stimulated violent internal dissension in the United States. Lacking clear national purpose, neutrality was the obvious policy.

The right road for America
These considerations, which became open and obvious during the war, applied equally to American policy in the years before. It is sometimes said on behalf of Theodore Roosevelt that he had a clearer sense of the importance of the European balance for the United States than had his contemporaries. For this there is almost no evidence. During his presidency opportunities to intervene in European affairs were few. He took those that offered and made the most of them in his usual ebullient way, clearly enjoying both the deference paid to him in Europe, and the feeling that he was enhancing the powers of the presidency. Yet it is hard to suppose that the course of events would have been different if he had done nothing at all. In the last resort he could not have persuaded his country into any dangerous or expensive course, and it is to his great credit that he knew it. When the European war broke out, Roosevelt was eager that the United States should join in at once on the Allied side. His dislike and scorn for Woodrow Wilson were enhanced by Wilson's resolute determination to stay neutral for as long as possible. Yet American interests

were best served by Wilson's course, not by Roosevelt's – unless it be argued, as it could hardly have been at the time, that the Russian Revolution, foreseen by none, would have been staved off by rapid Allied success.

This is a period in which we find American policy expounded in terms which conceal the essential realism of its practice. The leaders of the Progressive movement were men who tried to integrate foreign and domestic policy into a coherent whole. As they sought for greater discipline, unity, and order at home, so they hoped to advance these good ends abroad also. But though the general principle could easily be stated, its application was a matter of difficulty and divergence. American leaders could not help supposing that what was good for America was good for the world; and they were disappointed by opposition to their well-meant efforts. Some were more pessimistic than others, and so more inclined to think that the United States had to act; or, if they were more pessimistic still, that it was too late for action. In some areas action was easy – Latin America, for example. Yet in Latin America, despite the complaints of Latin Americans, what stands out is how moderate and half-hearted the policy of the United States has usually been.

Behind the difficulties of American policy lay certain salient and paradoxical facts – the enormous and growing power of the United States, and her geographical position. The power meant that the United States could always decide to act later. The last possible moment for action was reached only rarely and slowly. Until it was, a compelling case for immediate action was hard to make. The position of the United States meant that – except in Latin America – action always involved a large step. It meant jumping across a major ocean to act in lands on the other side. Given America's natural resources, the alternative policy of 'fortress America' always had attractions. The argument that some other part of the world was vital to the United States – vital in the sense that only war and not negotiation could protect American interests – was hard to make persuasive. Isolationism is an opprobrious term. To call American policy in these years isolationist suggests that there was a proper and different national policy which men of sense could have identified and followed. There was none. These were years in which Americans, having built their navy, were rightly content to wait and see.

Left: Ex-President Roosevelt with French General Dalstein who was military governor of Paris. Roosevelt's favourite role in foreign affairs was as an international 'honest broker'

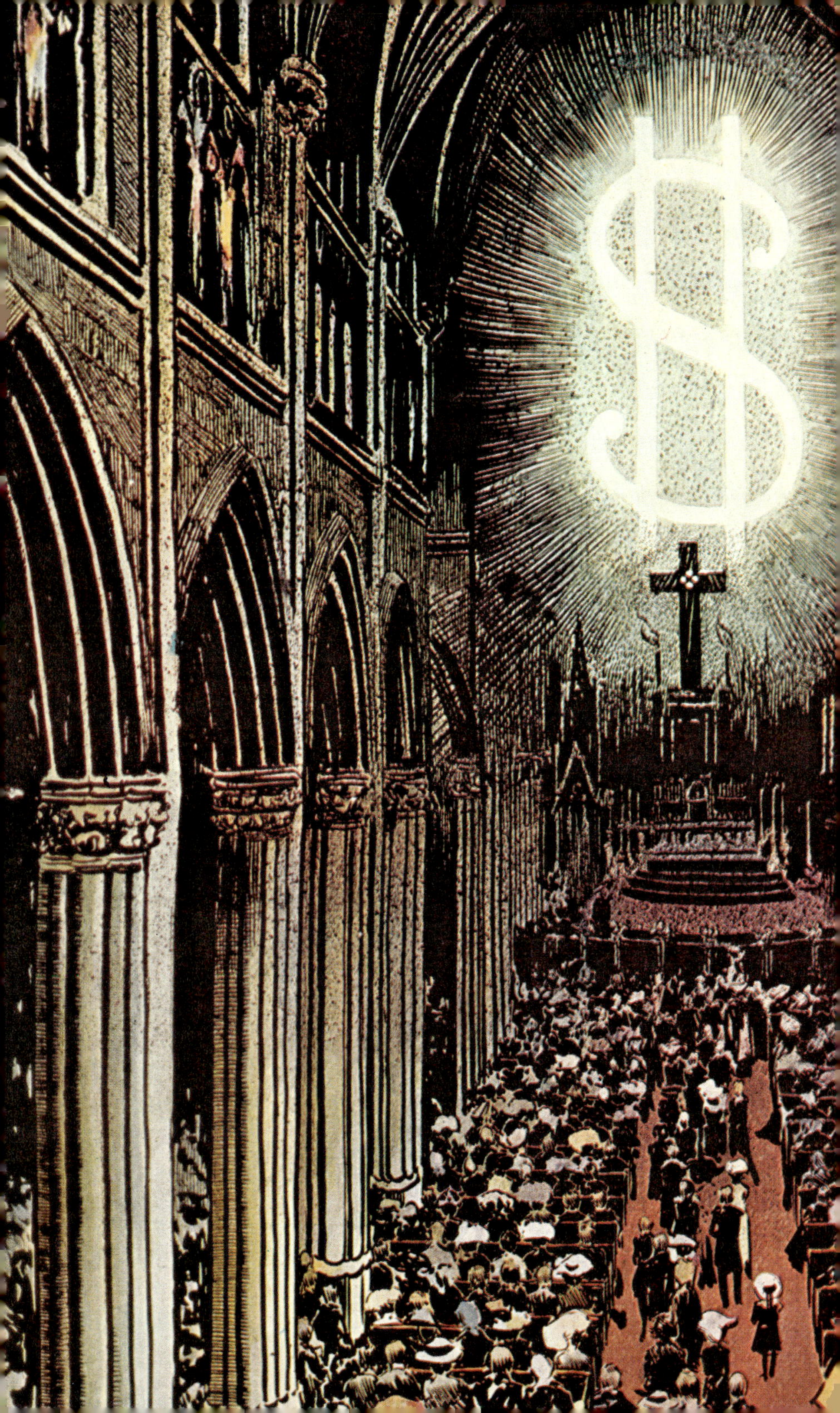

Chapter 7
The Decline of Progressivism

When Roosevelt left office in 1909, it was only to hand it over to his chosen successor, William Howard Taft. Taft, who easily retained the Republican grip on the presidency in the election of 1908, frustrating William Jennings Bryan in yet a third attempt to gain it, was a Progressive of long standing, and an old friend and colleague of Roosevelt. He had been an enlightened Governor of the Philippines, leaving to become Secretary of War during Roosevelt's second term. His Republican credentials were equally impressive, dating back to his appointment as Solicitor-General by President Harrison in the early 'nineties; and he came from a state—Ohio—known as a home of Republican presidents. Roosevelt departed for Africa to shoot big game, partly at least to get out of the way of his successor, and he left with cordial expressions of goodwill and esteem. Quite a lot of people were glad to see him go. Men tire readily of almost any political personality, and Roosevelt's was undeniably tiring. After nearly eight years, his energy had begun to seem frenzied and his exhortations shrill.

His successor could hardly have presented a greater contrast. Taft was a large, bulky man, urbane and genial. His talents were for negotiation and administration, not for politics. Though his Progressive sympathies were not in doubt, they were allied to a conservative temperament made more conservative by a legal training. 'Theodore', said one of his colleagues, 'was a bit of a bluffer occasionally, and at the same time he had nerve to go on—to take a chance his statements would have the deciding effect and, if not, to go on and trust the country would back him up....' Taft liked to be sure that what he was doing was both safe and legally correct. For example, when civil war broke out in Cuba in 1906, it became necessary to decide whether the United States should exercise a treaty right to intervene. Taft wanted to get a legal ruling from the Attorney-General, and possibly even a vote from Congress to support action. Roose-

Left: *Worshipping the holy dollar—against the Progressives' dream of a more just society stood the ancient vice of greed*

velt, by contrast, was determined to do neither of those things. One of the attractions of intervention for him was that, if the intervention were successful as he had no doubt it would be, it would strengthen the hands of future presidents by giving them a useful precedent. For Roosevelt the enlarging of presidential power—at least while he and his party held it—was an end in itself. For Taft it was not.

The battle for the tariff
The difference quickly proved critical. Taft took office with the advantage that both houses of Congress were controlled by his party. But that party was far from united; Taft's reluctance to offend either wing of his party gave too much power to the conservative old guard. As the Progressive wing protested, he found himself falling more and more under conservative influence without the self-confident vigour required to regain independence. The first major piece of evidence was his failure to accomplish tariff reform, which had been one of the Republican campaign promises. Although the platform had been, as usual, vague, reform had been generally understood to mean a lower tariff. That had also been Taft's personal understanding. He had long been in favour of a lower tariff. He had spoken out against the existing rates before his election—perhaps more courageously than wisely—and he called Congress into special session to consider the tariff immediately on taking office. Yet when the Payne-Aldritch Tariff Act of 1909 was passed, its effect was actually to raise the rates. The House made some small reductions. The Senate restored most of them, as well as striking out an inheritance tax which had been included in the House bill.

The intricacies of the process by which a tariff act was finally agreed between the two houses and passed into law are not for discussion here. By his own inclination, by the skill of the conservatives, especially Senator Aldritch, and, it should be added, by the folly of the Progressive leaders, Taft, though still struggling with some success to keep the rates down, had become identified with the Senate conservatives. Moreover, though inept in their congressional tactics, the Progressives were skilful in public relations. They contrived to represent the tariff as not merely an economic measure, as not merely a struggle for advantage among different regions dependent on different products, in which, on the whole, the primary-producing regions had been defeated and the manufacturing regions had won, but rather as a Wall Street conspiracy which the President, through folly or feebleness or treachery, had been unable to resist. In this kind of battle Taft was nearly helpless. He had neither skill nor stomach for it. And perhaps he valued the unity of the party even above his own reputation. In the event he lost both.

The same inability to muster support is seen in another area in which Taft's credentials are beyond question. He was more of a 'trust-buster' than Roosevelt had been. Where Roosevelt had invoked the Sherman Act from time to time, without much faith in its efficacy but with great public effect, Taft believed in it. He believed in competition and he believed in law. He brought more suits to dismantle trusts than Roosevelt had done, without gaining anything like the credit. One suit did him serious harm. He attacked the United States Steel Company, one of the greatest trusts. The suit did harm not because the government lost it, though it ultimately did, but because it fanned into furious hostility the distrust which had been growing between Taft and Roosevelt almost since Roosevelt's return from Africa. Part of the case against the company rested on its purchase in 1907 of a smaller steel company, which Roosevelt, then President, had allowed to pass unchallenged. He and Taft had discussed the matter, then and later, and Roosevelt had gained no sense of Taft's disapproval. When the purchase was made an issue in the suit, he felt both that Taft was acting dishonourably and that his own integrity was being called in question.

Though the suit dragged on with little effect on American industry, it was important because it threw the weight of Roosevelt against Taft. One of Taft's difficulties was that the party regulars, who were in a majority in Congress, and especially in the Senate, did not have the bulk of the country behind them. The Democrats made substantial gains in the mid-term elections of 1910, capturing control of the House of Representatives for the first time since 1895; and they did so by putting themselves forward as the party of reform. It began to look as if many Republican reformers would reject their own President in 1912. One possible alternative was Robert La Follette of Wisconsin, a notable Midwestern Republican Progressive leader. But La Follette had disadvantages. He was too identified with his own region to be altogether acceptable outside it. From the first, many of the rebels would have preferred Roosevelt. Roosevelt would have none of it. He privately believed that the Democrats were bound to win in 1912, whoever the Republican candidate was, and his habit of party regularity, forged over a lifetime, was not lightly broken. But he was so outraged by Taft's steel suit that he changed his mind, and contended with both Taft and La Follette for

Left: TR's protegé and successor in the presidency, 'Big Bill' Taft (seen here with Negro leader Booker T.Washington in 1906)

the Republican nomination. Taft won, and Roosevelt, in a burst of fury, decided to run independently as leader of the Progressive Party.

The struggle for the Republican nomination reveals how far Taft had already been identified as the spokesman of the conservatives. How did a man who had been one of Roosevelt's leading disciples come to be in such a position? Partly the answer must lie in Roosevelt's dominating personality. Roosevelt could persuade Taft into being a Progressive; deprived of that stimulus Taft became more conservative. But that is not the whole explanation, and we are reminded again how very various the Progressive movement was. Taft was a genuine Progressive – up to a point. After that point he thought the movement had gone far enough, and he stopped. But the movement did not stop. It continued to develop new and more radical demands. There was a still more fundamental sense in which Taft was a conservative. Even when he was reforming, his chosen *methods* of reform remained traditional. Perhaps that was most obvious in his liking for the courts as an instrument of equity. Though La Follette, the other Republican contender, was not conservative in that sense, he also represented reformers who were increasingly looking backwards. His style was old-fashioned, and he could not break out of the Midwestern regional mould.

Roosevelt had none of these disadvantages. Rather he became increasingly the spokesman of that wing of the Progressive movement which most looked to the future, the wing whose imagination had been captured by science in all its aspects, the science of government as well as technology. He recognised that the world of the future would be immensely more complex than the world of the past, and, as a man who in office had loved power and wielded it confidently, he concluded that a larger and more powerful part for government was required. He had begun to elaborate this soon after returning from Africa, in a famous speech of 1910 in which he coined the phrase which later became his campaign slogan: the 'new nationalism'.

While Roosevelt was failing to gain the Republican nomination, and forming the Progressive Party, the Democrats also were nominating a reform candidate, Woodrow Wilson, who, after an academic career culminating in the presidency of Princeton University, had made a dazzling debut in politics as Governor of New Jersey. The election of 1912 was three-cornered – Taft against Roosevelt against Wilson. It quickly became clear that the real contest was between Wilson and Roosevelt, with

Right: Teddy out of office – but still very much in the action

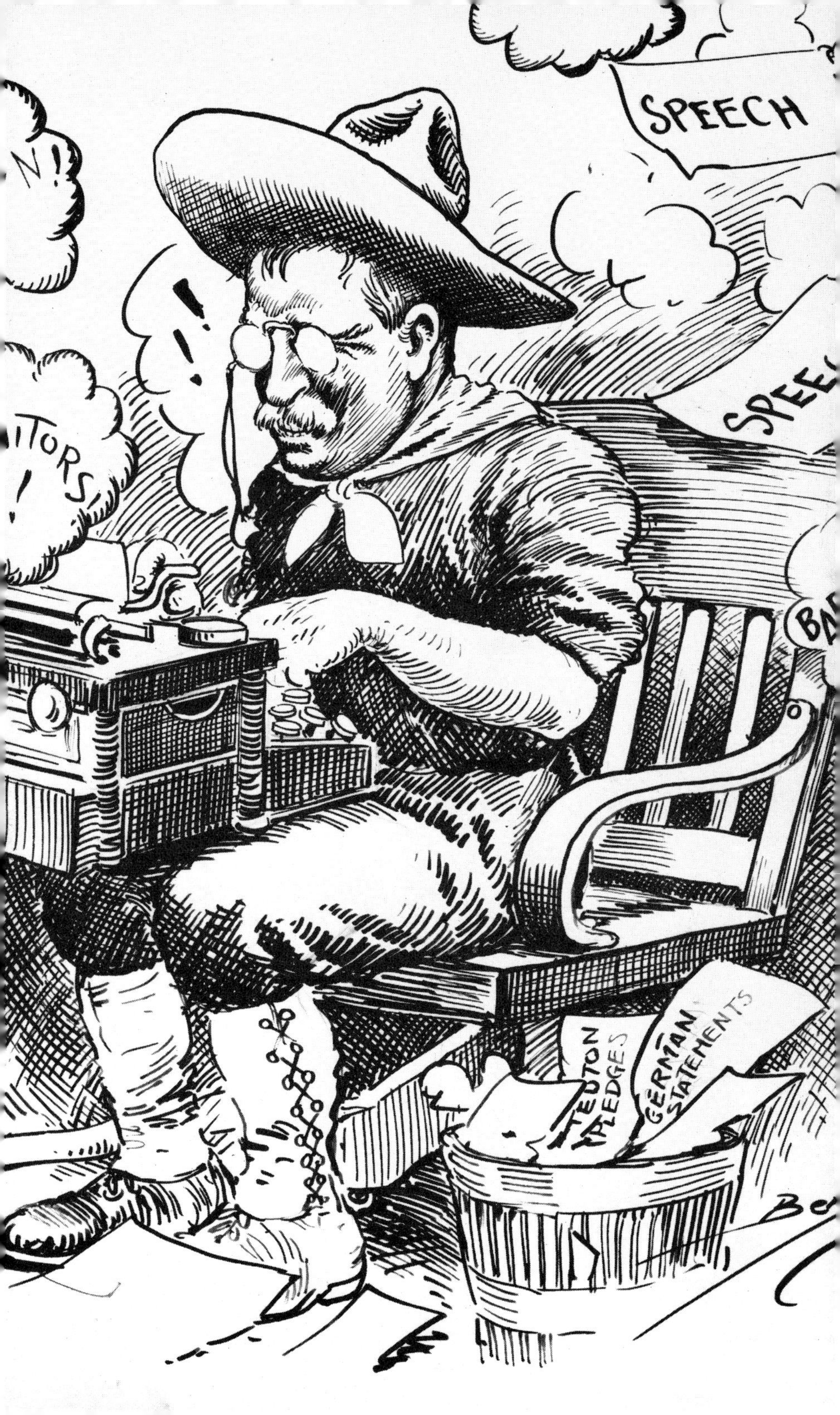
SPEECH
TEUTON PLEDGES
GERMAN STATEMENTS

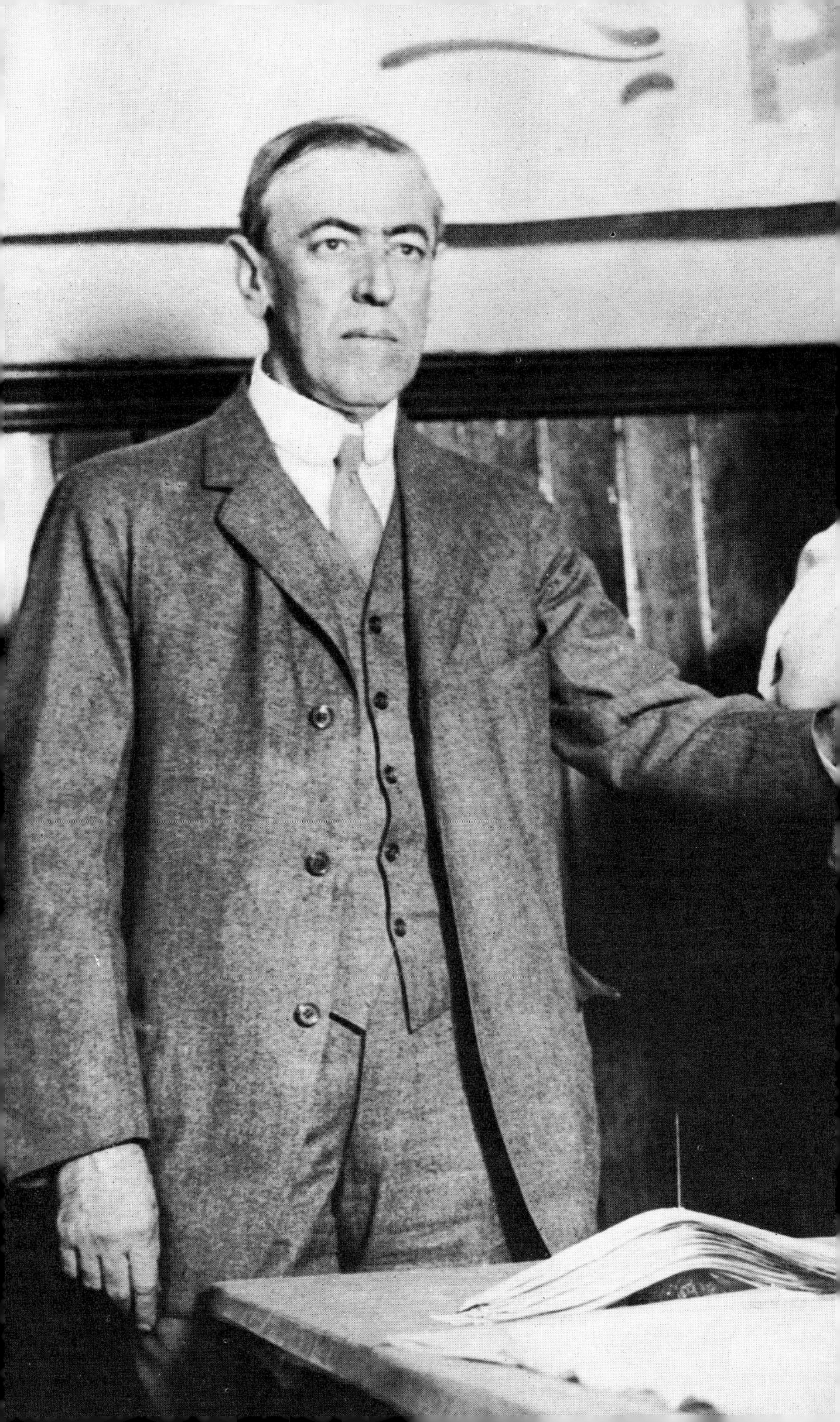

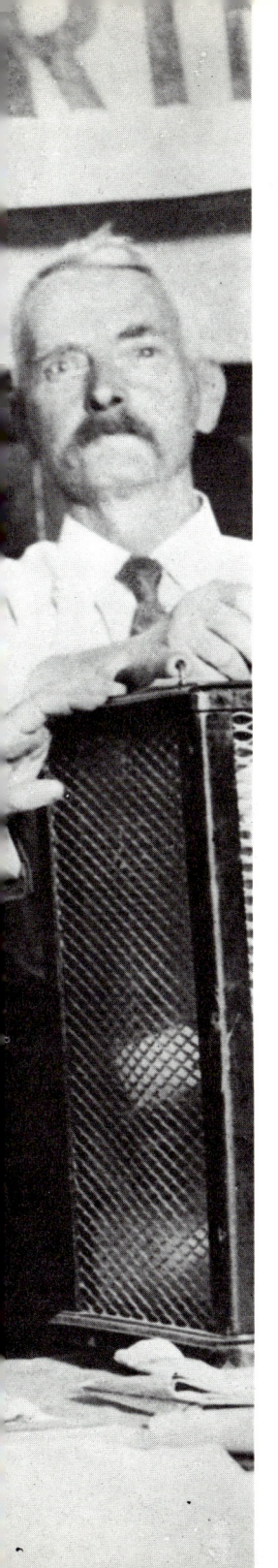

Taft a poor third. As the two avowed reformers contended, they elaborated the differences between Roosevelt's 'new nationalism' and Wilson's 'new freedom'.

The 'new freedom' was in many ways a sort of East Coast version of La Follette's Progressivism. As a Democrat Wilson had to rely on Southern supporters, and among these there were many who hankered for an older America of traditional rural virtues. Wilson himself, indeed, looked for a programme of limited reform which would put right abuses, restrict certain excesses, and then allow the government to return to the limited, regulatory role which it had played in the past. With the advantage of the Republican split, Wilson won the election easily. He gained only a minority of the popular vote, but that mattered little when he had a substantial majority in both houses of Congress, when the opposition party was not merely divided but hopelessly at loggerheads, and when Wilson's reform programme could win him support from independents. Wilson was a very different man from Roosevelt, and the two disliked each other to the point of hatred. Opposition, when confined to the formal channels of politics, brought out the best in Roosevelt. He abused his opponents furiously in private, and sometimes in public, but he became more ingenious and more thoughtful by reason of their opposition. Wilson declined under opposition. It made him stubborn, arrogant, and inflexible. But Wilson also had what Roosevelt had, and what Taft so sadly lacked – a zest for power which gave him both the determination and the capacity to use it. He was at his best on a wave of success; and that he had in his early years.

The 'new freedom' in action

Wilson's reform record in his first years was remarkable. In the Underwood Tariff Act of 1913 he actually succeeded in lowering the tariff. The establishment of the Federal Reserve System gave the government a degree of control over banking and currency which has grown ever since. The establishment of the Federal Trade Commission and the passing of the Clayton Anti-trust Act gave trust-busters more effective weapons than they had had under the old Sherman Act. Most important for the future, the passage of the Sixteenth Amendment to the Constitution in 1913 finally enabled Congress to impose a federal income tax. Yet effective though this programme was, it had an old-fashioned air. The banking regulations derived from an old Democratic tradition that the money supply should be controlled by the government and not by banks. Again, the tariff too was an old issue, and the

Left: The third man in the 1912 election – Woodrow Wilson

Democrats were bound to lower it when they came to power. Wilson's measures against trusts, also, were designed to break them up, rather than to control them. In essence, Wilson was looking back to the America of the small entrepreneur, the private man, which some thinkers already saw to be dying. The obverse of this attitude was that, in the early years, Wilson had little interest in positive measures of social reform. He had, indeed, the distrust of 'special' legislation which has so often been found in his section and in his party. Federal regulation of hours or wages or working conditions, for example, made little appeal to him. It is true that later, in 1916, he advanced a more radical programme, but he did so in response to public demand at a time when his own interest was already firmly centred on the war in Europe.

Reluctant warrior
It is ironic that Wilson should have been the man to lead America during the First World War. The traditions of his party, his own background, and his earlier career made him disinclined to take an interest in foreign affairs. Even his concern for the advancement of good government in Latin America was the product of missionary zeal which may have been misguided, but which owed little to any serious consideration of American national interest. His preference might have been for that neglect of foreign affairs from which the United States had only recently emerged. Inevitably, however, after 1914 the President became more and more preoccupied with the European war, and particularly with the problem of how to remain neutral as the war at sea became ever more intense. The problem of maintaining neutral rights during a major war was an old and intractable one. It had baffled American statesmen as far back as the Napoleonic period and had done much to bring on the War of 1812 with Britain. The development of the submarine gave it a new dimension. If the United States acquiesced in submarine warfare, her weight would be thrown against the Allies; if she made effective protest, it would be thrown against Germany. Meanwhile, although they did not take American lives, British restrictions were as damaging as submarines to American trade.

Wilson threaded his way through this labyrinth with splendid patience and ingenuity. He was not to be finally baffled until the Germans decided that unrestricted warfare, even if it forced an American declaration of war, would offer them their best hope of victory. Behind Wilson's labours for peace lay several considerations. Like any sensitive man, he was appalled by the horrors of the war, and hoped to spare his countrymen. He knew that Americans were as divided in their sympathies as they were mixed in their racial origins, and he foresaw how the country would be torn apart by involvement. He knew, moreover, that most people were anxious to stay out of the war. From time to time there were outbursts of public indignation, but the general temper remained pacific. In the election of 1916 one of Wilson's most effective slogans, though not one which he himself wanted to exploit, was 'He kept us out of war'. The public wanted peace not only for its own sake but because only in peacetime could prosperity and reform continue.

Meanwhile, the Republicans were still suffering from their split of 1912. Roosevelt, out of office and chafing at inaction, had become increasingly hysterical in his attacks on Wilson. Convinced that the United States should have joined the Allied side earlier in the war, he believed that the President's conduct was both inept and cowardly. Wilson was failing to defend American interests. It may be that in his analysis of the war Roosevelt was right—though it is far from certain. What is certain is that he was increasingly out of touch with American opinion. He hoped that he might again be a candidate in 1916. The Republican leaders would have none of him, and nominated Charles Evans Hughes, a distinguished candidate with a good reform record, and the Chief Justice of the Supreme Court. Hughes's task was formidable. Wilson had placed himself at the head of a reform coalition which now included the Democratic South, the farm radicals for whom Bryan had spoken, much of organised labour, and many of the most respected names of the Progressive movement—men who had worked for Roosevelt in 1912. And he had kept the country out of war. Against this Hughes, good man though he was, had to rely chiefly on the fact that the Republican Party was in normal times the majority party. Split in 1912, it had let Wilson in; reunited in 1916, it might throw him out. It nearly did. The election of 1916 was so close that the first results persuaded both candidates that Hughes had won. Hughes went to bed thinking he was President. He awoke to learn he was not.

Wilson's victory, then, was a victory for reform and for peace. But Wilson himself had long been aware that it might become necessary to intervene in the war and had done his best to prepare the country for intervention. As he had also foreseen, reform was the first war casualty. In 1917 the Progressive period came to an end. Though the power of the federal government inevitably increased during the war, and though such power once gained is never completely lost, post-war disillusionment undid much of the work of the Progressives.

Left: The 'Bull Moose' convention, 1912. Its platform—TR

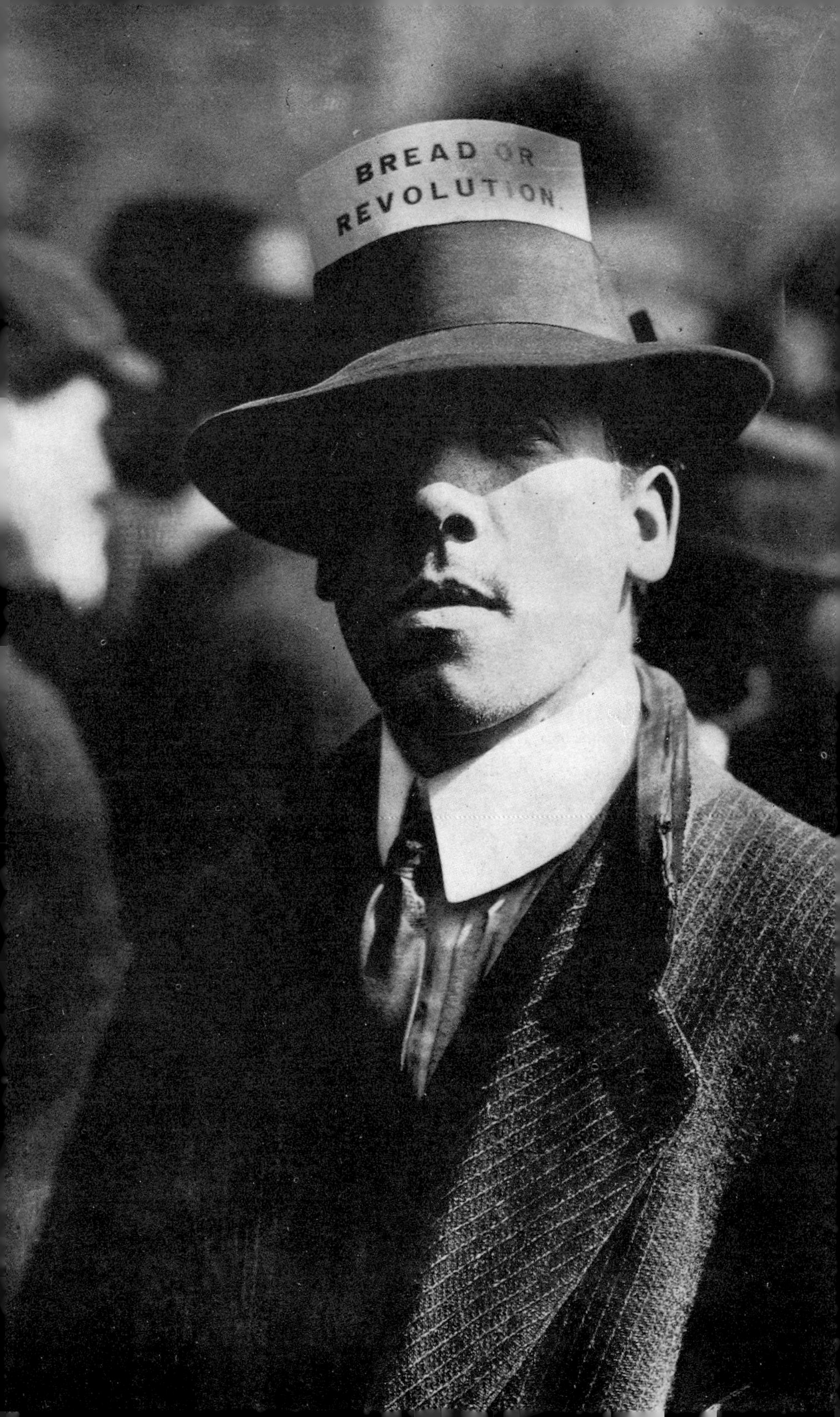
BREAD OR
REVOLUTION.

Epilogue
The Legacy

The Progressive period, broadly defined, covered the years from 1900 until America's entry into the First World War. It was shaped by two of the major political figures in American history, and by an unusual number of fascinating minor characters. For interest, certainly, it can hold its own. But of what permanent significance is it in the story of modern America? The Progressives won some victories and suffered some defeats. The impetus which they gave to American life died out in the 1920s. Their history is not a watershed, such as a war is, or a revolution, or a struggle for independence. It is one period in the continuing development of an open society, which retains a large capacity for making mistakes and a large capacity for repairing them. Yet the Progressive era has a larger significance. It was the period in which some Americans at least first came to recognise that continuing social change would call for continuing political adjustment.

The special difficulties of the Progressive era were created by the history of the preceding century. One subject of much concern to us today can be almost neglected in a study of the Progressive period, as in the study of the twenty years before and after it — race relations. The Negro was not a prominent national figure, nor were his problems identified as special. For that fact the men of the time are not to blame. They were entitled to deal with their problems; it is for us to deal with ours. But, if we may set on one side the problems of race relations, it can be argued that the Civil War drew a gigantic red herring across the path of American history.

Clearly the power of government was bound to grow. But the process might have taken a different and a more steady course if it had not been complicated by the sectional struggle deriving from slavery. For twenty years before the Civil War, and for thirty years after it, the federal government was reduced to a degree of helplessness unusual in Western states. The pressure for reform, when it

Left: *American revolutionary, 1914. Hard on the heels of Progressivism's decline came other, sterner philosophies*

came to a head, did so with a violence which now looks excessive, and provoked some demands which now seem eccentric.

Perhaps the most useful dividing line which we can draw among the Progressives is between those who saw reform as essentially a matter of correcting defects in an old structure which remained basically sound, and those who, realising that the world was changing and would change even faster in the future, saw also that in such a world there could be no resource save confident ingenuity. It is the great merit of Theodore Roosevelt that he placed himself firmly at the head of the second group. He was sure that what the United States needed, and that all the United States needed, was enough good and energetic men active in its public service. Roosevelt was not especially democratic. For him, patriotic Americans were those who gave him support. That mattered little, for the democratic conventions of America were powerful enough to keep even Roosevelt in check. What was important was that he saw Progressivism as a continuing and positive force. He was not alone in that, of course. It is from this period that we date the readiness of the Supreme Court to reinterpret the Constitution to meet the changing needs of an increasingly sophisticated society — a movement which Roosevelt approved and supported.

Roosevelt and Wilson belong together in American history much as Disraeli and Gladstone in British history. They were linked opposites. But of the two, the influence of Roosevelt is the more dominant, for we can say: 'No Roosevelt, no Wilson.' When Roosevelt took office, the Republican Party was established as the majority party, expecting to be in office most of the time. Roosevelt strengthened that expectation by making it the party of progress at a time when the odds were shifting against any conservative party. Yet by his choice of Taft to succeed him, by his quarrel with Taft, and by his decision to lead an independent party in 1912, he opened the way for Wilson to gain power.

In most respects Wilson was a more old-fashioned reformer than Roosevelt. There was, as Roosevelt claimed, a good deal of the rural tory about him. His vision of America and of America's world role was both more conservative and more limited than Roosevelt's. We do not know what course Wilson's career might have taken had it not been for the war in Europe. The war first made and then ruined him as, in an emotional sense, it ruined Roosevelt also. But Wilson's ultimate failure must not blind us to his competence as a politician. Aided by Roosevelt's continuing prestige and Roosevelt's increasing errors of judgement after 1910, he accomplished a result which has not yet been reversed. He took the role of reform party away from the Republicans and gave it to the Democrats. He began to forge the political coalition which Franklin Roosevelt was later to lead. In many ways the line of descent from Theodore to Franklin Roosevelt is extraordinarily close – but they belonged to different parties. That was Wilson's work. The Republicans who benefited from his rejection over the Treaty of Versailles were firmly stamped as conservatives. By then Theodore Roosevelt was dead.

'Supremely *there*'

In an open society the influence of individuals is not easy to judge. We are apt to suppose that what one man did, another man could equally have done. In terms of positive achievement, Roosevelt must rank below the greatest presidents, and even below Wilson. Yet his influence may have been as great, through his defects as much as through his merits. Suppose Roosevelt had not split the Republican Party in 1912. Should we assume that the course of reform would have been the same under Republican leadership as it has been under Democratic? The Republican Party, after all, owed nothing to Southern votes. Should we even assume that if Roosevelt's Progressive coalition had survived, the two-party system could have survived with it? The attrition of the Democratic Party, if continued a little longer, might have reduced it to impotence. But this is speculation. Largely because of his own defects, Roosevelt did not succeed in achieving the society he set out to build. But he saw it with a clearer vision and he goaded men towards it more effectively than anyone else.

If American history in the 19th century had not been distorted by slavery and secession, Roosevelt might not have been needed. Without his failings American history in the 20th century might have taken a very different course. Oliver Wendell Holmes, himself a towering figure on the Supreme Court for thirty years, once remarked: 'A great man represents a great ganglion in the nerves of society, or, to vary the figure, a strategic point in the campaign of history, and part of his greatness consists in his being *there*.' Roosevelt would have disliked the sentiment because it suggests that there are limits to what a man can accomplish, but it may stand both as his epitaph and as the reason for his importance. For good and ill alike he was supremely *there*. And if the continuing development of society has made much of his work out of date, he, more than any of his rivals and colleagues, would have recognised that process as inevitable and just.

Left: The verdict of his contemporaries (TR died in 1919)

Chronology of Events

1860 Abraham Lincoln is elected President
1861 The Civil War between North and South begins
1862 **22nd September:** Lincoln issues a proclamation declaring that from 1st January 1863 all slaves dwelling in the rebel states would be free
1865 The South is defeated; the Union preserved
14th April: Lincoln is shot by John Wilkes Booth. He dies on the following day and is succeeded by Andrew Johnson
1868 **24th February-26th May:** impeachment and trial of President Johnson by Congress; Johnson acquitted
1869 **26th February:** Fifteenth Amendment to the Constitution, which guarantees Negroes the right to vote, adopted by Congress
1873 Crédit Mobilier scandal
1889 Theodore Roosevelt is appointed to the Civil Service Commission
1890 **2nd July:** Sherman Anti-Trust Law enacted. The act forbade combinations in restraint of trade, and though designed to control business corporations, was later also used against labour unions
1897 Roosevelt appointed Assistant Secretary of the Navy
1898 **15th February:** USS *Maine* mysteriously blown up in Havana harbour
25th April: Congress declares that a state of war had existed since 21st April between the United States and Spain
1st July: Battle of San Juan Hill in Cuba; Roosevelt and his Rough Riders take part
10th December: Treaty of Paris ends war. Spain withdraws from Cuba and cedes Puerto Rico, Guam, and the Philippines to the United States
1900 **6th November:** Roosevelt elected Vice-President under William McKinley
1901 **6th September:** McKinley shot by an anarchist; dies 14th September and is succeeded by Roosevelt
1903 **18th November:** Hay-Bunau-Varilla Treaty grants the United States the use of a zone five miles wide on either side of the proposed Panama Canal
1904 **8th November:** Roosevelt elected to a second term
2nd December: Roosevelt enunciates his corollary to the Monroe Doctrine, warning Western hemisphere powers that if they are guilty of 'wrongdoing' the United States might feel compelled to intervene in their affairs
1905 Roosevelt offers his services as a mediator between Russia and Japan; conference opens at Portsmouth, New Hampshire on 9th August and a treaty of peace is signed on 5th September
1908 **3rd November:** William H. Taft is elected President
1912 **24th February:** Roosevelt announces he will accept the Republican nomination for President
22nd June: Republicans nominate Taft
7th August: Roosevelt nominated as candidate of the Progressive—or 'Bull Moose'—Party
5th November: Woodrow Wilson elected President
1917 **6th April:** United States declares war on Germany
1919 **6th January:** Roosevelt dies

Top: Roosevelt addresses Panama police force, 1906 (left); TR with Japanese delegates at the Portsmouth, New Hampshire peace conference which ended the Russo-Japanese War, 1905 (centre); painting of the explosion on the USS *Maine* in Havana harbour—the event which triggered off the Spanish-American War, 1898 (right). *Centre:* 1907 cartoon mocks the hopes of the Hague Peace Conference—Alexander, Caesar, and Napoleon chuckle over its deliberations (left); TR in a flying machine, 1910 (right). *Bottom:* The combative ex-President, 1910 (left); 'King Theodore'—a comment on his dominance of American life (centre); Gene Debs, Socialist leader (right)

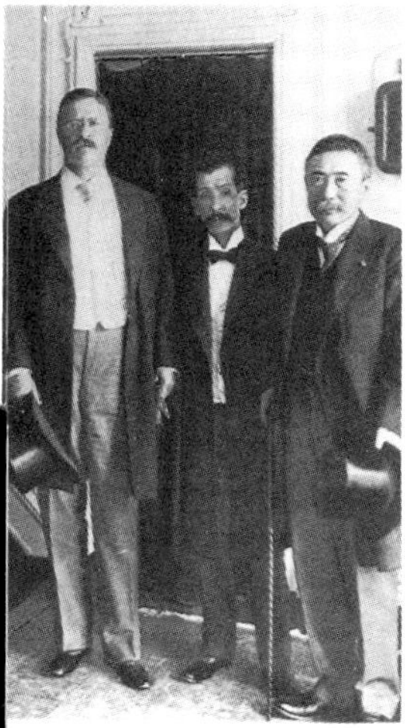

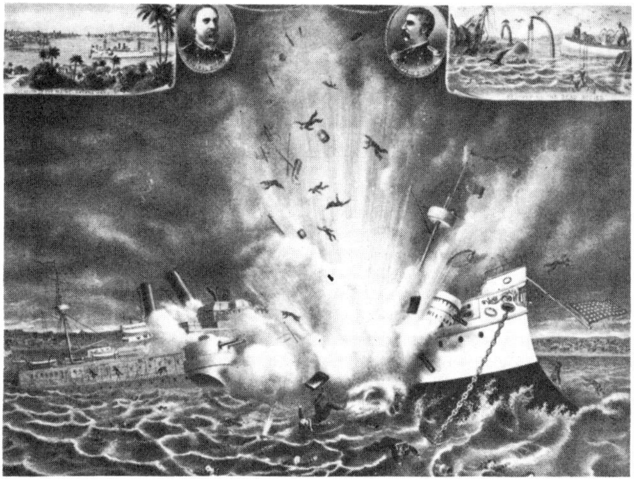

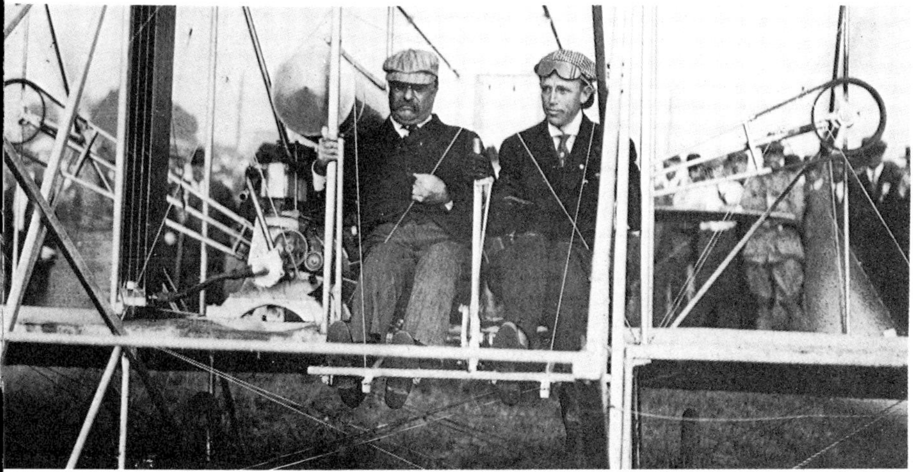

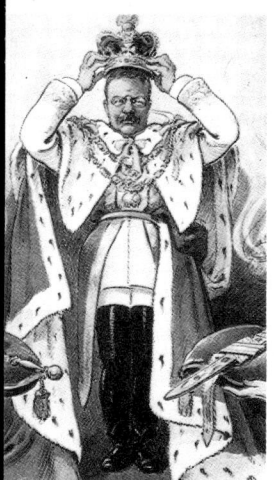

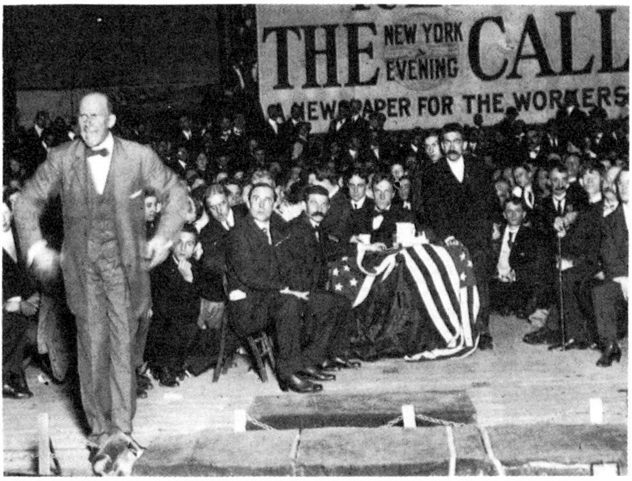
THE NEW YORK EVENING CALL

Index of main people, places, and events

Adams John Quincy 16-18
Addams Jane 61
Africa 109 111 112
West 14
Alaska 86 94
Aldritch Senator 110
American Association for the Advancement of Science 86
Federation of Labor 60
Railway Union 60
Revolution (1776-83) 11 14 93
Appomattox 38
Arizona 55
Armour Philip 37 38
Asia 95 100-6
Astor John Jacob 37
Atcheson, Topeka and Santa Fe Railroad 26
Atlantic Ocean 44 89 93 98 100
Austria-Hungary immigrants from 28
Baltimore and Ohio Railroad Company 18
Beveridge Senator 84
Birmingham Alabama 32
Blaine James G 51 65
Boers 5
Boxer Rising (1900) 101
Brandeis Louis 76
Britain 5 11 14 18 27 42 72 77 84 88 89 95 96 98-100 106 120
British immigrants 28
Bryan William Jennings 6 69 70 71 109 117
Bryce James 49
Buffalo Exposition (1909) 5
California 21 22
Canada 88
Cannon Joseph ('Uncle Joe') 81
Carnegie Andrew 37 39
Carey Land Act (1894) 88
Carolina South 19
Central Pacific Railroad Company 22-6
Charleston 19
Chicago 27 60 82
Exposition (1893) 5
Children's Bureau 61
Chilean Navy 98
China 71 101
Chinese immigrants 26
Civil Service Commission 50 65
Civil War (1861-65) 16 19 20 21 27 28 29 31 32 37 39 47 53 54 59 65 66 70 73 76 94 119
Clayton Anti-trust Act 115
Cleveland Grover 54 61 69 82 86
Colfax Schuyler, Vice-President of the USA 38
Columbia District of 83
Confederacy 19 20 31
Constitution 14 18 19 73-6 77 79 115 120
Cooke Jay 37
Crédit Mobilier 38

Cuba 66 69 94 95 96 109
Dakota Territory 65
Davis Jefferson 20
Debs Eugene 59
De Leon Daniel 59
Democratic Party 6 18 19 47 49 50 53 54 61 65 69 81 111 112 115 121
Dewey Commodore 95
Dingley Tariff Act (1897) 54
Disraeli Benjamin 120
'Dooley Mr' 67 77 95
Drew Daniel 38
DuBois WEB 45
Dunne Finlay Peter 67
Eisenhower Dwight 54
Elkins Act (1903) 84
Erie Canal 18
Farmers' Alliances 59
Federal Reserve System 115
Trade Commission 115
Forest Reserve Act (1891) 86
Fort Sumter 19
France 11 100
Garfield James 50
General Strike (1926) 84
German immigrants 11 28 106
liberal revolution (1848) 11
Germany 5 44 71 95 100 116
Gladstone William Ewart 120
Gompers Samuel 600
Gould Jay 37 60
Granger laws 73
movement 55-9
Grant Ulysses S 20 38 49 65
Great Exhibition (1851) 5
Lakes 11 18
Northern Railroad 26
Greeley Horace 49
Greenback movement 59
Party 51
Labor Party 51
Hanna Mark 69 70
Harlan Justice 76
Harriman EH 82
Harrison Benjamin 86 109
Harvard University 63
Havana 94
Hawaii 95
Hay John 5 101
Hayes Rutherford 50
Haymarket Riot (1886) 60
Hepburn Act (1906) 84
Hill James J 26 37 82
Holmes Oliver Wendell 76 82 121
Homestead Act (1862) 22
Hughes Charles Evans 117
Hull House 61
Hungarian immigrants 28
Illinois 59 81
Indians American 11
Indies West 32
Interstate Commerce Act (1887) 61
Iowa 21 59
Irish Famine (1846) 11
immigrants 11 26 28 106
Italian immigrants 28
Japan 93 95 100-1
Jefferson Thomas 79

124

Jewish immigrants 28
Johnson Andrew 20 49
Kelley Florence 61
Knights of Labor 59-60
Korea 100
La Follette Robert 111 112 115
Lathrop Julia 61
Latin America 107 116
Lee Robert E 38
Liberal Republican Party 49-50
Lincoln Abraham 8 19 20 21
Lloyd HD 60
Long John D 66
Maine 81
Maine 94
Manchuria 100 101
Manila 95
Massachusetts 76
McKinley William 61 67 69-70 71 82 86
Tariff Act (1890) 53
Milwaukee 27
Minnesota 21
Mississippi River 11 18 21 31
Missouri River 22
Mitchell John 6 84
Monroe James 98
Morgan John Pierpont 37 39 82
Morocco crisis (1905) 89
National Association for the Advancement of Coloured People 45
Grange of the Patrons of Husbandry 55-9
Negroes 11-14 16 31 32 45 76 119 121
New England 44
New Jersey 112
New Orleans 32
New York City 50 59 63 66
State 18 50 67
Northern Pacific Railroad 26
Securities Company 82
Ohio 50 109
Omaha 22
Oregon 21
Pacific Ocean 89 98 100
Panama Canal 100
Zone 89 100
Republic of 100
Payne-Aldritch Tariff Act (1909) 110
Peking 101
Pennsylvania 18 28 84
Railroad 26
Philadelphia 59
Philippines 95-6 100 109
Pinchot Gifford 86
Pittsburgh 28
Platt Senator TC 67
Polish immigrants 28
Populist Revolt (1892-6) 69-70
Portsmouth Treaty of (1905) 89
Powderly Terence 60
Princeton University 112
Progressive movement 7-8 39 51 60 67-9 70-2 77 79 81 83 86 107 109 110 112 117 119
Party 112
Promontory Point Utah 26

Radical Republicans 20 73 81
Reclamation Act (1902) 88
Reed TB ('Tsar') 81
Republican Party 19 20 47 49-50 51 61 65 66 67 69 109 112 115 117 120 121
Resumption Act (1875) 51
Rockefeller John D 29 37 39
Rocky Mountains 26
Roosevelt Franklin 8 121
Theodore 8 61 63-9 70 77 79 81-2 83 84 86 88-9 100 106-7 109-10 111-15 117 120 121
Theodore (father of 'TR') 63
'Rough Riders' 66-7
Russia 71 94 100 101
Russian immigrants 28 106
Revolution (1917) 107
Russo-Japanese War (1904-5) 89 100
Scandinavian immigrants 28
Seward William Henry, Secretary of State 94
Sherman Act (1890) 82 83 111 115
Sierra Nevada California 26
Social Democratic Party 59
Socialist Labor Party 59
Party 59
Spain 5 11 94 95
Spanish-American War (1898) 5-6 66 94
Standard Oil 29 39 60
Superior Lake 26 27
Taft William Howard 109 110-11 112 115 120
Texas and Pacific Railroad 26
Tilden Samuel 50
Toynbee Hall London 61
Tweed Ring 50
Underwood Tariff Act (1913) 115
Union Pacific Railroad Company 22-6 38
United Mineworkers of America 84
United States Army 94
Navy 66 94-5 101 107
Steel Company 39 111
Utah 26
Vanderbilt 'Commodore' Cornelius 37
Versailles Treaty of (1919) 88 121
Wald Lillian 61
War of 1812 116
Washington D.C. 66
Washington George 8
Whig Party 18-19 47
Wilhelm II Kaiser of Germany 89
Wilson-Gorman Tariff Act (1894) 53 54
Wilson Woodrow 8 76 79 88 106-7 112-15 116-17 120-1
Wisconsin 21 59 111
World War First 8 29 45 60 106 116 119

125

Author's suggestions for further reading

The best recent single volume surveying the whole period is RH Wiebe, *The Search for Order, 1877-1920* (1967). The New American Nation Series contains two admirable volumes—GE Mowry, *The Era of Theodore Roosevelt, 1900-1912* (1958) and AS Link, *Woodrow Wilson and the Progressive Era, 1910-1917* (1954)—both with very full bibliographies.

EC Kirkland, *Industry Comes of Age, 1860-1897* (1961) and FA Shannon, *The Farmer's Last Frontier, 1860-1897* (1945) are two standard works on different aspects of economic history. To these may be added TC Cochran and W Miller, *The Age of Enterprise* (revised ed. 1961) and M Josephson, *The Robber Barons* (2nd ed. 1962).

The Chicago History of American Civilization series includes JP Stover, *American Railroads* (1961); MA Jones, *American Immigration* (1960); and H Pelling, *American Labor* (1960).

JD Hicks, *The Populist Revolt* (1931), though challenged by later writers, has yet to be superseded. CM Destler, *American Radicalism, 1865-1901* (1946) is a good survey, and R Hofstadter, *The Age of Reform* (1955) is perceptive and provocative.

On foreign policy FR Dulles, *America's Rise to World Power* (1955) is sound and comprehensive; ER May, *American Imperialism* (1968) discusses the domestic roots of American policy; and so does W LaFeber, *The New Empire, 1860-1898* (1963), which emphasises, indeed overemphasises, the economic motives for expansion.

Finally, the most recent full length study of Roosevelt is by WH Harbaugh, *Power and Responsibility: the Life and Times of Theodore Roosevelt* (1961); but no one should overlook the brilliant short essay by JM Blum, *The Republican Roosevelt* (1954).

Library of the 20th Century will include the following titles:

Russia in Revolt
David Floyd
The Second Reich
Harold Kurtz
The Anarchists
Roderick Kedward
Suffragettes International
Trevor Lloyd
War by Time-Table
AJP Taylor
Death of a Generation
Alistair Horne
Suicide of the Empires
Alan Clark
Twilight of the Habsburgs
ZAB Zeman
Early Aviation
Sir Robert Saundby
Birth of the Movies
DJ Wenden
America Comes of Age
AE Campbell
Lenin's Russia
G Katkov
The Weimar Republic
Sefton Delmer
Out of the Lion's Paw
Constantine Fitzgibbon
Japan: The Years of Triumph
Louis Allen
Communism Takes China
CP FitzGerald
Black and White in South Africa
GH Le May
Woodrow Wilson
RH Ferrell
France 1918-34
W Knapp
France 1934-40
AN Wahl
Mussolini's Italy
Geoffrey Warner
The Little Dictators
A Polonsky
Viva Zapata
L Bethell
The World Depression
Malcolm Falkus
Stalin's Russia
A Nove
The Brutal Reich
Donald Watt
The Spanish Civil War
Raymond Carr
Munich: Czech Tragedy
KG Robbins